TREATY OF AMSTERDAM AMENDING THE TREATY ON EUROPEAN UNION, THE TREATIES ESTABLISHING THE EUROPEAN COMMUNITIES AND CERTAIN RELATED ACTS

INTRODUCTORY NOTE

This publication reproduces the text of the Treaty of Amsterdam amending the Treaty on European Union, the Treaties establishing the European Communities and certain related acts, as signed in Amsterdam on 2 October 1997.

The text has been produced for documentary purposes and does not involve the responsibility of the institutions

A great deal of additional information on the European Union is available on the Internet. It can be accessed through the Europa server (http://europa.eu.int)

Cataloguing data can be found at the end of this publication

Luxembourg: Office for Official Publications of the European Communities, 1997

ISBN 92-828-1652-4

Printed in Germany

CONTENTS (not part of the Treaty)

HIS MAJESTY THE KING OF THE BELGIANS,

HER MAJESTY THE QUEEN OF DENMARK,

THE PRESIDENT OF THE FEDERAL REPUBLIC OF GERMANY,

THE PRESIDENT OF THE HELLENIC REPUBLIC,

HIS MAJESTY THE KING OF SPAIN,

THE PRESIDENT OF THE FRENCH REPUBLIC,

THE COMMISSION AUTHORISED BY ARTICLE 14 OF THE CONSTITUTION OF IRELAND TO EXERCISE AND PERFORM THE POWERS AND FUNCTIONS OF THE PRESIDENT OF IRELAND,

THE PRESIDENT OF THE ITALIAN REPUBLIC,

HIS ROYAL HIGHNESS THE GRAND DUKE OF LUXEMBOURG,

HER MAJESTY THE QUEEN OF THE NETHERLANDS,

THE FEDERAL PRESIDENT OF THE REPUBLIC OF AUSTRIA,

THE PRESIDENT OF THE PORTUGUESE REPUBLIC,

THE PRESIDENT OF THE REPUBLIC OF FINLAND,

HIS MAJESTY THE KING OF SWEDEN,

HER MAJESTY THE QUEEN OF THE UNITED KINGDOM OF GREAT BRITAIN AND NORTHERN IRELAND,

HAVE RESOLVED to amend the Treaty on European Union, the Treaties establishing the European Communities and certain related acts,

and to this end have designated as their Plenipotentiaries:

HIS MAJESTY THE KING OF THE BELGIANS:

Mr. Erik Derycke,
Minister for Foreign Affairs;

HER MAJESTY THE QUEEN OF DENMARK:

Mr. Niels Helveg Petersen,
Minister for Foreign Affairs;

THE PRESIDENT OF THE FEDERAL REPUBLIC OF GERMANY:

Dr. Klaus Kinkel,
Federal Minister for Foreign Affairs
and Deputy Federal Chancellor;

THE PRESIDENT OF THE HELLENIC REPUBLIC:

Mr. Theodoros Pangalos,
Minister for Foreign Affairs;

HIS MAJESTY THE KING OF SPAIN:

Mr. Juan Abel Matutes,
Minister for Foreign Affairs;

THE PRESIDENT OF THE FRENCH REPUBLIC:

Mr. Hubert Védrine,
Minister for Foreign Affairs;

THE COMMISSION AUTHORISED BY ARTICLE 14 OF THE CONSTITUTION OF IRELAND TO EXERCISE AND PERFORM THE POWERS AND FUNCTIONS OF THE PRESIDENT OF IRELAND:

Mr. Raphael P. Burke,
Minister for Foreign Affairs;

THE PRESIDENT OF THE ITALIAN REPUBLIC:

Mr. Lamberto Dini,
Minister for Foreign Affairs;

HIS ROYAL HIGHNESS THE GRAND DUKE OF LUXEMBOURG:

Mr. Jacques F. Poos,
Deputy Prime Minister,
Minister for Foreign Affairs, Foreign Trade and Cooperation;

HER MAJESTY THE QUEEN OF THE NETHERLANDS:

Mr. Hans van Mierlo,
Deputy Prime Minister
and Minister for Foreign Affairs;

THE FEDERAL PRESIDENT OF THE REPUBLIC OF AUSTRIA:

Mr. Wolfgang Schüssel,
Federal Minister for Foreign Affairs
and Vice Chancellor;

THE PRESIDENT OF THE PORTUGUESE REPUBLIC:

Mr. Jaime Gama,
Minister for Foreign Affairs;

THE PRESIDENT OF THE REPUBLIC OF FINLAND:

Ms. Tarja Halonen,
Minister for Foreign Affairs;

HIS MAJESTY THE KING OF SWEDEN:

Ms. Lena Hjelm-Wallén,
Minister for Foreign Affairs;

HER MAJESTY THE QUEEN OF THE UNITED KINGDOM OF GREAT BRITAIN AND
NORTHERN IRELAND:

Mr. Douglas Henderson,
Minister of State,
Foreign and Commonwealth Office;

WHO, having exchanged their full powers found in good and due form,

HAVE AGREED AS FOLLOWS:

PART ONE

SUBSTANTIVE AMENDMENTS

Article 1

The Treaty on European Union shall be amended in accordance with the provisions of this Article.

1. After the third recital the following recital shall be inserted:

    'CONFIRMING their attachment to fundamental social rights as defined in the European Social Charter signed at Turin on 18 October 1961 and in the 1989 Community Charter of the Fundamental Social Rights of Workers,'

2. The existing seventh recital shall be replaced by the following:

    'DETERMINED to promote economic and social progress for their peoples, taking into account the principle of sustainable development and within the context of the accomplishment of the internal market and of reinforced cohesion and environmental protection, and to implement policies ensuring that advances in economic integration are accompanied by parallel progress in other fields,'

3. The existing ninth and tenth recitals shall be replaced by the following:

    'RESOLVED to implement a common foreign and security policy including the progressive framing of a common defence policy, which might lead to a common defence in accordance with the provisions of Article J.7, thereby reinforcing the European identity and its independence in order to promote peace, security and progress in Europe and in the world,

    RESOLVED to facilitate the free movement of persons, while ensuring the safety and security of their peoples, by establishing an area of freedom, security and justice, in accordance with the provisions of this Treaty,'

4. In Article A the second paragraph shall be replaced by the following:

    'This Treaty marks a new stage in the process of creating an ever closer union among the peoples of Europe, in which decisions are taken as openly as possible and as closely as possible to the citizen.'

5. Article B shall be replaced by the following:

    '**Article B**

    The Union shall set itself the following objectives:

    — to promote economic and social progress and a high level of employment and to achieve balanced and sustainable development, in particular through the creation of an area without internal frontiers, through the strengthening of economic and social cohesion and through the establishment of economic and monetary union, ultimately including a single currency in accordance with the provisions of this Treaty;

— to assert its identity on the international scene, in particular through the implementation of a common foreign and security policy including the progressive framing of a common defence policy, which might lead to a common defence, in accordance with the provisions of Article J.7;

— to strengthen the protection of the rights and interests of the nationals of its Member States through the introduction of a citizenship of the Union;

— to maintain and develop the Union as an area of freedom, security and justice, in which the free movement of persons is assured in conjunction with appropriate measures with respect to external border controls, asylum, immigration and the prevention and combating of crime;

— to maintain in full the *acquis communautaire* and build on it with a view to considering to what extent the policies and forms of cooperation introduced by this Treaty may need to be revised with the aim of ensuring the effectiveness of the mechanisms and the institutions of the Community.

The objectives of the Union shall be achieved as provided in this Treaty and in accordance with the conditions and the timetable set out therein while respecting the principle of subsidiarity as defined in Article 3b of the Treaty establishing the European Community.'

6. In Article C, the second paragraph shall be replaced by the following:

'The Union shall in particular ensure the consistency of its external activities as a whole in the context of its external relations, security, economic and development policies. The Council and the Commission shall be responsible for ensuring such consistency and shall cooperate to this end. They shall ensure the implementation of these policies, each in accordance with its respective powers.'

7. Article E shall be replaced by the following:

'**Article E**

The European Parliament, the Council, the Commission, the Court of Justice and the Court of Auditors shall exercise their powers under the conditions and for the purposes provided for, on the one hand, by the provisions of the Treaties establishing the European Communities and of the subsequent Treaties and Acts modifying and supplementing them and, on the other hand, by the other provisions of this Treaty.'

8. Article F shall be amended as follows:

(a) paragraph 1 shall be replaced by the following:

'1.   The Union is founded on the principles of liberty, democracy, respect for human rights and fundamental freedoms, and the rule of law, principles which are common to the Member States.';

(b) the existing paragraph 3 shall become paragraph 4 and a new paragraph 3 shall be inserted as follows:

'3.   The Union shall respect the national identities of its Member States.'

9. The following Article shall be inserted at the end of Title I:

'**Article F.1**

1.   The Council, meeting in the composition of the Heads of State or Government and acting by unanimity on a proposal by one third of the Member States or by the Commission and after obtaining the assent of the European Parliament, may determine the existence of a serious and persistent breach by a Member State of principles mentioned in Article F(1), after inviting the government of the Member State in question to submit its observations.

2.   Where such a determination has been made, the Council, acting by a qualified majority, may decide to suspend certain of the rights deriving from the application of this Treaty to the Member State in question, including the voting rights of the representative of the government of that Member State in the Council. In doing so, the Council shall take into account the possible consequences of such a suspension on the rights and obligations of natural and legal persons.

The obligations of the Member State in question under this Treaty shall in any case continue to be binding on that State.

3.   The Council, acting by a qualified majority, may decide subsequently to vary or revoke measures taken under paragraph 2 in response to changes in the situation which led to their being imposed.

4.   For the purposes of this Article, the Council shall act without taking into account the vote of the representative of the government of the Member State in question. Abstentions by members present in person or represented shall not prevent the adoption of decisions referred to in paragraph 1. A qualified majority shall be defined as the same proportion of the weighted votes of the members of the Council concerned as laid down in Article 148(2) of the Treaty establishing the European Community.

This paragraph shall also apply in the event of voting rights being suspended pursuant to paragraph 2.

5.   For the purposes of this Article, the European Parliament shall act by a two thirds majority of the votes cast, representing a majority of its members.'

10. Title V shall be replaced by the following:

'Title V

PROVISIONS ON A COMMON FOREIGN AND SECURITY POLICY

Article J.1

1.   The Union shall define and implement a common foreign and security policy covering all areas of foreign and security policy, the objectives of which shall be:

— to safeguard the common values, fundamental interests, independence and integrity of the Union in conformity with the principles of the United Nations Charter;

— to strengthen the security of the Union in all ways;

— to preserve peace and strengthen international security, in accordance with the principles of the United Nations Charter, as well as the principles of the Helsinki Final Act and the objectives of the Paris Charter, including those on external borders;

— to promote international cooperation;

— to develop and consolidate democracy and the rule of law, and respect for human rights and fundamental freedoms.

2.   The Member States shall support the Union's external and security policy actively and unreservedly in a spirit of loyalty and mutual solidarity.

The Member States shall work together to enhance and develop their mutual political solidarity. They shall refrain from any action which is contrary to the interests of the Union or likely to impair its effectiveness as a cohesive force in international relations.

The Council shall ensure that these principles are complied with.

Article J.2

The Union shall pursue the objectives set out in Article J.1 by:

— defining the principles of and general guidelines for the common foreign and security policy;

— deciding on common strategies;

— adopting joint actions;

— adopting common positions;

— strengthening systematic cooperation between Member States in the conduct of policy.

Article J.3

1.   The European Council shall define the principles of and general guidelines for the common foreign and security policy, including for matters with defence implications.

2.   The European Council shall decide on common strategies to be implemented by the Union in areas where the Member States have important interests in common.

Common strategies shall set out their objectives, duration and the means to be made available by the Union and the Member States.

3.   The Council shall take the decisions necessary for defining and implementing the common foreign and security policy on the basis of the general guidelines defined by the European Council.

The Council shall recommend common strategies to the European Council and shall implement them, in particular by adopting joint actions and common positions.

The Council shall ensure the unity, consistency and effectiveness of action by the Union.

Article J.4

1.   The Council shall adopt joint actions. Joint actions shall address specific situations where operational action by the Union is deemed to be required. They shall lay down their objectives, scope, the means to be made available to the Union, if necessary their duration, and the conditions for their implementation.

2.   If there is a change in circumstances having a substantial effect on a question subject to joint action, the Council shall review the principles and objectives of that action and take the necessary decisions. As long as the Council has not acted, the joint action shall stand.

3.   Joint actions shall commit the Member States in the positions they adopt and in the conduct of their activity.

4.   The Council may request the Commission to submit to it any appropriate proposals relating to the common foreign and security policy to ensure the implementation of a joint action.

5.   Whenever there is any plan to adopt a national position or take national action pursuant to a joint action, information shall be provided in time to allow, if necessary, for prior consultations within the Council. The obligation to provide prior information shall not apply to measures which are merely a national transposition of Council decisions.

6.   In cases of imperative need arising from changes in the situation and failing a Council decision, Member States may take the necessary measures as a matter of urgency having regard to the general objectives of the joint action. The Member State concerned shall inform the Council immediately of any such measures.

7.   Should there be any major difficulties in implementing a joint action, a Member State shall refer them to the Council which shall discuss them and seek appropriate solutions. Such solutions shall not run counter to the objectives of the joint action or impair its effectiveness.

Article J.5

The Council shall adopt common positions. Common positions shall define the approach of the Union to a particular matter of a geographical or thematic nature. Member States shall ensure that their national policies conform to the common positions.

Article J.6

Member States shall inform and consult one another within the Council on any matter of foreign and security policy of general interest in order to ensure that the Union's influence is exerted as effectively as possible by means of concerted and convergent action.

Article J.7

1.   The common foreign and security policy shall include all questions relating to the security of the Union, including the progressive framing of a common defence policy, in accordance with the second subparagraph, which might lead to a common defence, should the European Council so decide. It shall in that case recommend to the Member States the adoption of such a decision in accordance with their respective constitutional requirements.

The Western European Union (WEU) is an integral part of the development of the Union providing the Union with access to an operational capability notably in the context of paragraph 2. It supports the Union in framing the defence aspects of the common foreign and security policy as set out in this Article. The Union shall accordingly foster closer institutional relations with the WEU with a view to the possibility of the integration of the WEU into the Union, should the European Council so decide. It shall in that case recommend to the Member States the adoption of such a decision in accordance with their respective constitutional requirements.

The policy of the Union in accordance with this Article shall not prejudice the specific character of the security and defence policy of certain Member States and shall respect the obligations of certain Member States, which see their common defence realised in the North Atlantic Treaty Organisation (NATO), under the North Atlantic Treaty and be compatible with the common security and defence policy established within that framework.

The progressive framing of a common defence policy will be supported, as Member States consider appropriate, by cooperation between them in the field of armaments.

2.   Questions referred to in this Article shall include humanitarian and rescue tasks, peace-keeping tasks and tasks of combat forces in crisis management, including peace-making.

3.   The Union will avail itself of the WEU to elaborate and implement decisions and actions of the Union which have defence implications.

The competence of the European Council to establish guidelines in accordance with Article J.3 shall also obtain in respect of the WEU for those matters for which the Union avails itself of the WEU.

When the Union avails itself of the WEU to elaborate and implement decisions of the Union on the tasks referred to in paragraph 2 all Member States of the Union shall be entitled to participate fully in the tasks in question. The Council, in agreement with the institutions of the WEU, shall adopt the necessary practical arrangements to allow all Member States contributing to the tasks in question to participate fully and on an equal footing in planning and decision taking in the WEU.

Decisions having defence implications dealt with under this paragraph shall be taken without prejudice to the policies and obligations referred to in paragraph 1, third subparagraph.

4. The provisions of this Article shall not prevent the development of closer co-operation between two or more Member States on a bilateral level, in the framework of the WEU and the Atlantic Alliance, provided such cooperation does not run counter to or impede that provided for in this Title.

5. With a view to furthering the objectives of this Article, the provisions of this Article will be reviewed in accordance with Article N.

Article J.8

1. The Presidency shall represent the Union in matters coming within the common foreign and security policy.

2. The Presidency shall be responsible for the implementation of decisions taken under this Title; in that capacity it shall in principle express the position of the Union in international organisations and international conferences.

3. The Presidency shall be assisted by the Secretary-General of the Council who shall exercise the function of High Representative for the common foreign and security policy.

4. The Commission shall be fully associated in the tasks referred to in paragraphs 1 and 2. The Presidency shall be assisted in those tasks if need be by the next Member State to hold the Presidency.

5. The Council may, whenever it deems it necessary, appoint a special representative with a mandate in relation to particular policy issues.

Article J.9

1. Member States shall coordinate their action in international organisations and at international conferences. They shall uphold the common positions in such fora.

In international organisations and at international conferences where not all the Member States participate, those which do take part shall uphold the common positions.

2. Without prejudice to paragraph 1 and Article J.4(3), Member States represented in international organisations or international conferences where not all the Member States participate shall keep the latter informed of any matter of common interest.

Member States which are also members of the United Nations Security Council will concert and keep the other Member States fully informed. Member States which are permanent members of the Security Council will, in the execution of their functions, ensure the defence of the positions and the interests of the Union, without prejudice to their responsibilities under the provisions of the United Nations Charter.

Article J.10

The diplomatic and consular missions of the Member States and the Commission Delegations in third countries and international conferences, and their representations to international organisations, shall cooperate in ensuring that the common positions and joint actions adopted by the Council are complied with and implemented.

They shall step up cooperation by exchanging information, carrying out joint assessments and contributing to the implementation of the provisions referred to in Article 8c of the Treaty establishing the European Community.

Article J.11

The Presidency shall consult the European Parliament on the main aspects and the basic choices of the common foreign and security policy and shall ensure that the views of the European Parliament are duly taken into consideration. The European Parliament shall be kept regularly informed by the Presidency and the Commission of the development of the Union's foreign and security policy.

The European Parliament may ask questions of the Council or make recommendations to it. It shall hold an annual debate on progress in implementing the common foreign and security policy.

Article J.12

1. Any Member State or the Commission may refer to the Council any questions relating to the common foreign and security policy and may submit proposals to the Council.

2. In cases requiring a rapid decision, the Presidency, of its own motion, or at the request of the Commission or a Member State, shall convene an extraordinary Council meeting within forty-eight hours or, in an emergency, within a shorter period.

Article J.13

1. Decisions under this Title shall be taken by the Council acting unanimously. Abstentions by members present in person or represented shall not prevent the adoption of such decisions.

When abstaining in a vote, any member of the Council may qualify its abstention by making a formal declaration under the present subparagraph. In that case, it shall not be obliged to apply the decision, but shall accept that the decision commits the Union. In a spirit of mutual solidarity, the Member State concerned shall refrain from any action likely to conflict with or impede Union action based on that decision and the other Member States shall respect its position. If the members of the Council qualifying their abstention in this way represent more than one third of the votes weighted in accordance with Article 148(2) of the Treaty establishing the European Community, the decision shall not be adopted.

2. By derogation from the provisions of paragraph 1, the Council shall act by qualified majority:

— when adopting joint actions, common positions or taking any other decision on the basis of a common strategy;

— when adopting any decision implementing a joint action or a common position.

If a member of the Council declares that, for important and stated reasons of national policy, it intends to oppose the adoption of a decision to be taken by qualified majority, a vote shall not be taken. The Council may, acting by a qualified majority, request that the matter be referred to the European Council for decision by unanimity.

The votes of the members of the Council shall be weighted in accordance with Article 148(2) of the Treaty establishing the European Community. For their adoption, decisions shall require at least 62 votes in favour, cast by at least 10 members.

This paragraph shall not apply to decisions having military or defence implications.

3.   For procedural questions, the Council shall act by a majority of its members.

Article J.14

When it is necessary to conclude an agreement with one or more States or international organisations in implementation of this Title, the Council, acting unanimously, may authorise the Presidency, assisted by the Commission as appropriate, to open negotiations to that effect. Such agreements shall be concluded by the Council acting unanimously on a recommendation from the Presidency. No agreement shall be binding on a Member State whose representative in the Council states that it has to comply with the requirements of its own constitutional procedure; the other members of the Council may agree that the agreement shall apply provisionally to them.

The provisions of this Article shall also apply to matters falling under Title VI.

Article J.15

Without prejudice to Article 151 of the Treaty establishing the European Community, a Political Committee shall monitor the international situation in the areas covered by the common foreign and security policy and contribute to the definition of policies by delivering opinions to the Council at the request of the Council or on its own initiative. It shall also monitor the implementation of agreed policies, without prejudice to the responsibility of the Presidency and the Commission.

Article J.16

The Secretary-General of the Council, High Representative for the common foreign and security policy, shall assist the Council in matters coming within the scope of the common foreign and security policy, in particular through contributing to the formulation, preparation and implementation of policy decisions, and, when appropriate and acting on behalf of the Council at the request of the Presidency, through conducting political dialogue with third parties.

Article J.17

The Commission shall be fully associated with the work carried out in the common foreign and security policy field.

Article J.18

1.   Articles 137, 138, 139 to 142, 146, 147, 150 to 153, 157 to 163, 191a and 217 of the Treaty establishing the European Community shall apply to the provisions relating to the areas referred to in this Title.

2.   Administrative expenditure which the provisions relating to the areas referred to in this Title entail for the institutions shall be charged to the budget of the European Communities.

3.   Operational expenditure to which the implementation of those provisions gives rise shall also be charged to the budget of the European Communities, except for such expenditure arising from operations having military or defence implications and cases where the Council acting unanimously decides otherwise.

In cases where expenditure is not charged to the budget of the European Communities it shall be charged to the Member States in accordance with the gross national product scale, unless the Council acting unanimously decides otherwise. As for expenditure arising from operations having military or defence implications, Member States whose representatives in the Council have made a formal declaration under Article J.13(1), second subparagraph, shall not be obliged to contribute to the financing thereof.

4.   The budgetary procedure laid down in the Treaty establishing the European Community shall apply to the expenditure charged to the budget of the European Communities.'

11. Title VI shall be replaced by the following:

'Title VI

PROVISIONS ON POLICE AND JUDICIAL COOPERATION IN CRIMINAL MATTERS

Article K.1

Without prejudice to the powers of the European Community, the Union's objective shall be to provide citizens with a high level of safety within an area of freedom, security and justice by developing common action among the Member States in the fields of police and judicial cooperation in criminal matters and by preventing and combating racism and xenophobia.

That objective shall be achieved by preventing and combating crime, organised or otherwise, in particular terrorism, trafficking in persons and offences against children, illicit drug trafficking and illicit arms trafficking, corruption and fraud, through:

— closer cooperation between police forces, customs authorities and other competent authorities in the Member States, both directly and through the European Police Office (Europol), in accordance with the provisions of Articles K.2 and K.4;

— closer cooperation between judicial and other competent authorities of the Member States in accordance with the provisions of Articles K.3(a) to (d) and K.4;

— approximation, where necessary, of rules on criminal matters in the Member States, in accordance with the provisions of Article K.3(e).

Article K.2

1.   Common action in the field of police cooperation shall include:

(a) operational cooperation between the competent authorities, including the police, customs and other specialised law enforcement services of the Member States in relation to the prevention, detection and investigation of criminal offences;

(b) the collection, storage, processing, analysis and exchange of relevant information, including information held by law enforcement services on reports on suspicious financial transactions, in particular through Europol, subject to appropriate provisions on the protection of personal data;

(c) cooperation and joint initiatives in training, the exchange of liaison officers, secondments, the use of equipment, and forensic research;

(d) the common evaluation of particular investigative techniques in relation to the detection of serious forms of organised crime.

2.   The Council shall promote cooperation through Europol and shall in particular, within a period of five years after the date of entry into force of the Treaty of Amsterdam:

(a) enable Europol to facilitate and support the preparation, and to encourage the co-ordination and carrying out, of specific investigative actions by the competent authorities of the Member States, including operational actions of joint teams comprising representatives of Europol in a support capacity;

(b) adopt measures allowing Europol to ask the competent authorities of the Member States to conduct and coordinate their investigations in specific cases and to develop specific expertise which may be put at the disposal of Member States to assist them in investigating cases of organised crime;

(c) promote liaison arrangements between prosecuting/investigating officials specialising in the fight against organised crime in close cooperation with Europol;

(d) establish a research, documentation and statistical network on cross-border crime.

Article K.3

Common action on judicial cooperation in criminal matters shall include:

(a) facilitating and accelerating cooperation between competent ministries and judicial or equivalent authorities of the Member States in relation to proceedings and the enforcement of decisions;

(b) facilitating extradition between Member States;

(c) ensuring compatibility in rules applicable in the Member States, as may be necessary to improve such cooperation;

(d) preventing conflicts of jurisdiction between Member States;

(e) progressively adopting measures establishing minimum rules relating to the constituent elements of criminal acts and to penalties in the fields of organised crime, terrorism and illicit drug trafficking.

Article K.4

The Council shall lay down the conditions and limitations under which the competent authorities referred to in Articles K.2 and K.3 may operate in the territory of another Member State in liaison and in agreement with the authorities of that State.

Article K.5

This Title shall not affect the exercise of the responsibilities incumbent upon Member States with regard to the maintenance of law and order and the safeguarding of internal security.

Article K.6

1. In the areas referred to in this Title, Member States shall inform and consult one another within the Council with a view to coordinating their action. To that end, they shall establish collaboration between the relevant departments of their administrations.

2. The Council shall take measures and promote cooperation, using the appropriate form and procedures as set out in this Title, contributing to the pursuit of the objectives of the Union. To that end, acting unanimously on the initiative of any Member State or of the Commission, the Council may:

(a) adopt common positions defining the approach of the Union to a particular matter;

(b) adopt framework decisions for the purpose of approximation of the laws and regulations of the Member States. Framework decisions shall be binding upon the Member States as to the result to be achieved but shall leave to the national authorities the choice of form and methods. They shall not entail direct effect;

(c) adopt decisions for any other purpose consistent with the objectives of this Title, excluding any approximation of the laws and regulations of the Member States. These decisions shall be binding and shall not entail direct effect; the Council, acting by a qualified majority, shall adopt measures necessary to implement those decisions at the level of the Union;

(d) establish conventions which it shall recommend to the Member States for adoption in accordance with their respective constitutional requirements. Member States shall begin the procedures applicable within a time limit to be set by the Council.

Unless they provide otherwise, conventions shall, once adopted by at least half of the Member States, enter into force for those Member States. Measures implementing conventions shall be adopted within the Council by a majority of two-thirds of the Contracting Parties.

3. Where the Council is required to act by a qualified majority, the votes of its members shall be weighted as laid down in Article 148(2) of the Treaty establishing the European Community, and for their adoption acts of the Council shall require at least 62 votes in favour, cast by at least 10 members.

4. For procedural questions, the Council shall act by a majority of its members.

Article K.7

1. The Court of Justice of the European Communities shall have jurisdiction, subject to the conditions laid down in this Article, to give preliminary rulings on the validity and interpretation of framework decisions, and decisions on the interpretation of conventions established under this Title and on the validity and interpretation of the measures implementing them.

2. By a declaration made at the time of signature of the Treaty of Amsterdam or at any time thereafter, any Member State shall be able to accept the jurisdiction of the Court of Justice to give preliminary rulings as specified in paragraph 1.

3. A Member State making a declaration pursuant to paragraph 2 shall specify that either:

(a) any court or tribunal of that State against whose decisions there is no judicial remedy under national law may request the Court of Justice to give a preliminary ruling on a question raised in a case pending before it and concerning the validity or interpretation of an act referred to in paragraph 1 if that court or tribunal considers that a decision on the question is necessary to enable it to give judgment, or

(b) any court or tribunal of that State may request the Court of Justice to give a preliminary ruling on a question raised in a case pending before it and concerning the validity or interpretation of an act referred to in paragraph 1 if that court or tribunal considers that a decision on the question is necessary to enable it to give judgment.

4. Any Member State, whether or not it has made a declaration pursuant to paragraph 2, shall be entitled to submit statements of case or written observations to the Court in cases which arise under paragraph 1.

5. The Court of Justice shall have no jurisdiction to review the validity or proportionality of operations carried out by the police or other law enforcement services of a Member State or the exercise of the responsibilities incumbent upon Member States with regard to the maintenance of law and order and the safeguarding of internal security.

6.   The Court of Justice shall have jurisdiction to review the legality of framework decisions and decisions in actions brought by a Member State or the Commission on grounds of lack of competence, infringement of an essential procedural requirement, infringement of this Treaty or of any rule of law relating to its application, or misuse of powers. The proceedings provided for in this paragraph shall be instituted within two months of the publication of the measure.

7.   The Court of Justice shall have jurisdiction to rule on any dispute between Member States regarding the interpretation or the application of acts adopted under Article K.6(2) whenever such dispute cannot be settled by the Council within six months of its being referred to the Council by one of its members. The Court shall also have jurisdiction to rule on any dispute between Member States and the Commission regarding the interpretation or the application of conventions established under Article K.6(2)(d).

Article K.8

1.   A Coordinating Committee shall be set up consisting of senior officials. In addition to its coordinating role, it shall be the task of the Committee to:

— give opinions for the attention of the Council, either at the Council's request or on its own initiative;

— contribute, without prejudice to Article 151 of the Treaty establishing the European Community, to the preparation of the Council's discussions in the areas referred to in Article K.1.

2.   The Commission shall be fully associated with the work in the areas referred to in this Title.

Article K.9

Within international organisations and at international conferences in which they take part, Member States shall defend the common positions adopted under the provisions of this Title.

Articles J.8 and J.9 shall apply as appropriate to matters falling under this Title.

Article K.10

Agreements referred to in Article J.14 may cover matters falling under this Title.

Article K.11

1.   The Council shall consult the European Parliament before adopting any measure referred to in Article K.6(2)(b), (c) and (d). The European Parliament shall deliver its opinion within a time-limit which the Council may lay down, which shall not be less than three months. In the absence of an opinion within that time-limit, the Council may act.

2.   The Presidency and the Commission shall regularly inform the European Parliament of discussions in the areas covered by this Title.

3.   The European Parliament may ask questions of the Council or make recommendations to it. Each year, it shall hold a debate on the progress made in the areas referred to in this Title.

Article K.12

1.   Member States which intend to establish closer cooperation between themselves may be authorised, subject to Articles K.15 and K.16, to make use of the institutions, procedures and mechanisms laid down by the Treaties provided that the cooperation proposed:

(a) respects the powers of the European Community, and the objectives laid down by this Title;

(b) has the aim of enabling the Union to develop more rapidly into an area of freedom, security and justice.

2.   The authorisation referred to in paragraph 1 shall be granted by the Council, acting by a qualified majority at the request of the Member States concerned and after inviting the Commission to present its opinion; the request shall also be forwarded to the European Parliament.

If a member of the Council declares that, for important and stated reasons of national policy, it intends to oppose the granting of an authorisation by qualified majority, a vote shall not be taken. The Council may, acting by a qualified majority, request that the matter be referred to the European Council for decision by unanimity.

The votes of the members of the Council shall be weighted in accordance with Article 148(2) of the Treaty establishing the European Community. For their adoption, decisions shall require at least 62 votes in favour, cast by at least 10 members.

3.   Any Member State which wishes to become a party to cooperation set up in accordance with this Article shall notify its intention to the Council and to the Commission, which shall give an opinion to the Council within three months of receipt of that notification, possibly accompanied by a recommendation for such specific arrangements as it may deem necessary for that Member State to become a party to the cooperation in question. Within four months of the date of that notification, the Council shall decide on the request and on such specific arrangements as it may deem necessary. The decision shall be deemed to be taken unless the Council, acting by a qualified majority, decides to hold it in abeyance; in this case, the Council shall state the reasons for its decision and set a deadline for re-examining it. For the purposes of this paragraph, the Council shall act under the conditions set out in Article K.16.

4.   The provisions of Articles K.1 to K.13 shall apply to the closer cooperation provided for by this Article, save as otherwise provided for in this Article and in Articles K.15 and K.16.

The provisions of the Treaty establishing the European Community concerning the powers of the Court of Justice of the European Communities and the exercise of those powers shall apply to paragraphs 1, 2 and 3.

5.   This Article is without prejudice to the provisions of the Protocol integrating the Schengen *acquis* into the framework of the European Union.

Article K.13

1.   Articles 137, 138, 138e, 139 to 142, 146, 147, 148(3), 150 to 153, 157 to 163, 191a and 217 of the Treaty establishing the European Community shall apply to the provisions relating to the areas referred to in this Title.

2.   Administrative expenditure which the provisions relating to the areas referred to in this Title entail for the institutions shall be charged to the budget of the European Communities.

3.   Operational expenditure to which the implementation of those provisions gives rise shall also be charged to the budget of the European Communities, except where the Council acting unanimously decides otherwise. In cases where expenditure is not charged to the budget of the European Communities it shall be charged to the Member States in accordance with the gross national product scale, unless the Council acting unanimously decides otherwise.

4.   The budgetary procedure laid down in the Treaty establishing the European Community shall apply to the expenditure charged to the budget of the European Communities.

Article K.14

The Council, acting unanimously on the initiative of the Commission or a Member State, and after consulting the European Parliament, may decide that action in areas referred to in Article K.1 shall fall under Title IIIa of the Treaty establishing the European Community, and at the same time determine the relevant voting conditions relating to it. It shall recommend the Member States to adopt that decision in accordance with their respective constitutional requirements.'

12. The following new Title shall be inserted:

'Title VIa

PROVISIONS ON CLOSER COOPERATION

Article K.15

1.   Member States which intend to establish closer cooperation between themselves may make use of the institutions, procedures and mechanisms laid down by this Treaty and the Treaty establishing the European Community provided that the cooperation:

(a) is aimed at furthering the objectives of the Union and at protecting and serving its interests;

(b) respects the principles of the said Treaties and the single institutional framework of the Union;

(c) is only used as a last resort, where the objectives of the said Treaties could not be attained by applying the relevant procedures laid down therein;

(d) concerns at least a majority of Member States;

(e) does not affect the *acquis communautaire* and the measures adopted under the other provisions of the said Treaties;

(f) does not affect the competences, rights, obligations and interests of those Member States which do not participate therein;

(g) is open to all Member States and allows them to become parties to the cooperation at any time, provided that they comply with the basic decision and with the decisions taken within that framework;

(h) complies with the specific additional criteria laid down in Article 5a of the Treaty establishing the European Community and Article K.12 of this Treaty, depending on the area concerned, and is authorised by the Council in accordance with the procedures laid down therein.

2.   Member States shall apply, as far as they are concerned, the acts and decisions adopted for the implementation of the cooperation in which they participate. Member States not participating in such cooperation shall not impede the implementation thereof by the participating Member States.

Article K.16

1.   For the purposes of the adoption of the acts and decisions necessary for the implementation of the cooperation referred to in Article K.15, the relevant institutional provisions of this Treaty and of the Treaty establishing the European Community shall apply. However, while all members of the Council shall be able to take part in the deliberations, only those representing participating Member States shall take part in the adoption of decisions. The qualified majority shall be defined as the same proportion of the weighted votes of the members of the Council concerned as laid down in Article 148(2) of the Treaty establishing the European Community. Unanimity shall be constituted by only those Council members concerned.

2.   Expenditure resulting from implementation of the cooperation, other than administrative costs entailed for the institutions, shall be borne by the participating Member States, unless the Council, acting unanimously, decides otherwise.

Article K.17

The Council and the Commission shall regularly inform the European Parliament of the development of closer cooperation established on the basis of this Title.'

13. Article L shall be replaced by the following:

'Article L

The provisions of the Treaty establishing the European Community, the Treaty establishing the European Coal and Steel Community and the Treaty establishing the European Atomic Energy Community concerning the powers of the Court of Justice of the

European Communities and the exercise of those powers shall apply only to the following provisions of this Treaty:

(a) provisions amending the Treaty establishing the European Economic Community with a view to establishing the European Community, the Treaty establishing the European Coal and Steel Community and the Treaty establishing the European Atomic Energy Community;

(b) provisions of Title VI, under the conditions provided for by Article K.7;

(c) provisions of Title VIa, under the conditions provided for by Article 5a of the Treaty establishing the European Community and Article K.12 of this Treaty;

(d) Article F(2) with regard to action of the institutions, insofar as the Court has jurisdiction under the Treaties establishing the European Communities and under this Treaty;

(e) Articles L to S.'

14. In Article N, paragraph 2 shall be deleted and paragraph 1 shall remain without a number.

15. In Article O, the first paragraph shall be replaced by the following:

'Any European State which respects the principles set out in Article F(1) may apply to become a member of the Union. It shall address its application to the Council, which shall act unanimously after consulting the Commission and after receiving the assent of the European Parliament, which shall act by an absolute majority of its component members.'

16. In Article S, a new paragraph shall be added as follows:

'Pursuant to the 1994 Accession Treaty, the Finnish and Swedish versions of this Treaty shall also be authentic.'

Article 2

The Treaty establishing the European Community shall be amended in accordance with the provisions of this Article.

1. In the preamble the following recital shall be inserted after the eighth recital:

'DETERMINED to promote the development of the highest possible level of knowledge for their peoples through a wide access to education and through its continuous updating,'

2. Article 2 shall be replaced by the following:

'*Article 2*

The Community shall have as its task, by establishing a common market and an economic and monetary union and by implementing common policies or activities referred to in Articles 3 and 3a, to promote throughout the Community a harmonious, balanced and sustainable development of economic activities, a high level of employment and of social protection, equality between men and women, sustainable and non-inflationary growth, a high degree of competitiveness and convergence of economic performance, a high level of protection and improvement of the quality of the environment, the raising of the standard of living and quality of life, and economic and social cohesion and solidarity among Member States.'

3. Article 3 shall be amended as follows:

    (a) the existing text shall be numbered and become paragraph 1;

    (b) in new paragraph 1, point (d) shall be replaced by the following:

        '(d) measures concerning the entry and movement of persons as provided for in Title IIIa;';

    (c) in new paragraph 1, the following new point (i) shall be inserted after point (h):

        '(i) the promotion of coordination between employment policies of the Member States with a view to enhancing their effectiveness by developing a coordinated strategy for employment;'

    (d) in new paragraph 1, the existing point (i) shall become point (j) and the subsequent points shall be renumbered accordingly;

    (e) the following paragraph shall be added:

        '2.   In all the activities referred to in this Article, the Community shall aim to eliminate inequalities, and to promote equality, between men and women.'

4. The following Article shall be inserted:

'*Article 3c*

Environmental protection requirements must be integrated into the definition and implementation of the Community policies and activities referred to in Article 3, in particular with a view to promoting sustainable development.'

5. The following Article shall be inserted:

'*Article 5a*

1.   Member States which intend to establish closer cooperation between themselves may be authorised, subject to Articles K.15 and K.16 of the Treaty on the European Union, to make use of the institutions, procedures and mechanisms laid down by this Treaty, provided that the cooperation proposed:

    (a) does not concern areas which fall within the exclusive competence of the Community;

    (b) does not affect Community policies, actions or programmes;

    (c) does not concern the citizenship of the Union or discriminate between nationals of Member States;

    (d) remains within the limits of the powers conferred upon the Community by this Treaty; and

    (e) does not constitute a discrimination or a restriction of trade between Member States and does not distort the conditions of competition between the latter.

2.   The authorisation referred to in paragraph 1 shall be granted by the Council, acting by a qualified majority on a proposal from the Commission and after consulting the European Parliament.

If a member of the Council declares that, for important and stated reasons of national policy, it intends to oppose the granting of an authorisation by qualified majority, a vote shall not be taken. The Council may, acting by a qualified majority, request that the matter be referred to the Council, meeting in the composition of the Heads of State or Government, for decision by unanimity.

Member States which intend to establish closer cooperation as referred to in paragraph 1 may address a request to the Commission, which may submit a proposal to the Council to that effect. In the event of the Commission not submitting a proposal, it shall inform the Member States concerned of the reasons for not doing so.

3. Any Member State which wishes to become a party to cooperation set up in accordance with this Article shall notify its intention to the Council and to the Commission, which shall give an opinion to the Council within three months of receipt of that notification. Within four months of the date of that notification, the Commission shall decide on it and on such specific arrangements as it may deem necessary.

4. The acts and decisions necessary for the implementation of cooperation activities shall be subject to all the relevant provisions of this Treaty, save as otherwise provided for in this Article and in Articles K.15 and K.16 of the Treaty on European Union.

5. This Article is without prejudice to the provisions of the Protocol integrating the Schengen *acquis* into the framework of the European Union.'

6. In Article 6, the second paragraph shall be replaced by the following:

'The Council, acting in accordance with the procedure referred to in Article 189b, may adopt rules designed to prohibit such discrimination.'

7. The following Article shall be inserted:

'*Article 6a*

Without prejudice to the other provisions of this Treaty and within the limits of the powers conferred by it upon the Community, the Council, acting unanimously on a proposal from the Commission and after consulting the European Parliament, may take appropriate action to combat discrimination based on sex, racial or ethnic origin, religion or belief, disability, age or sexual orientation.'

8. The following Article shall be inserted at the end of Part One:

'*Article 7d*

Without prejudice to Articles 77, 90 and 92, and given the place occupied by services of general economic interest in the shared values of the Union as well as their role in promoting social and territorial cohesion, the Community and the Member States, each within their respective powers and within the scope of application of this Treaty, shall take care that such services operate on the basis of principles and conditions which enable them to fulfil their missions.'

9. Article 8(1) shall be replaced by the following:

'1.   Citizenship of the Union is hereby established. Every person holding the nationality of a Member State shall be a citizen of the Union. Citizenship of the Union shall complement and not replace national citizenship.'

10. Article 8a(2) shall be replaced by the following:

'2.   The Council may adopt provisions with a view to facilitating the exercise of the rights referred to in paragraph 1; save as otherwise provided in this Treaty, the Council shall act in accordance with the procedure referred to in Article 189b. The Council shall act unanimously throughout this procedure.'

11. In Article 8d, the following paragraph shall be added:

'Every citizen of the Union may write to any of the institutions or bodies referred to in this Article or in Article 4 in one of the languages mentioned in Article 248 and have an answer in the same language.'

12. Article 51 shall be replaced by the following:

'*Article 51*

The Council shall, acting in accordance with the procedure referred to in Article 189b, adopt such measures in the field of social security as are necessary to provide freedom of movement for workers; to this end, it shall make arrangements to secure for migrant workers and their dependants:

(a) aggregation, for the purpose of acquiring and retaining the right to benefit and of calculating the amount of benefit, of all periods taken into account under the laws of the several countries;

(b) payment of benefits to persons resident in the territories of Member States.

The Council shall act unanimously throughout the procedure referred to in Article 189b.'

13. Article 56(2) shall be replaced by the following:

'2.   The Council shall, acting in accordance with the procedure referred to in Article 189b, issue directives for the coordination of the abovementioned provisions.'

14. Article 57(2) shall be replaced by the following:

'2.   For the same purpose, the Council shall, acting in accordance with the procedure referred to in Article 189b, issue directives for the coordination of the provisions laid down by law, regulation or administrative action in Member States concerning the taking-up and pursuit of activities as self-employed persons. The Council, acting unanimously throughout the procedure referred to in Article 189b, shall decide on directives the implementation of which involves in at least one Member State amendment of the existing principles laid down by law governing the professions with respect to training and conditions of access for natural persons. In other cases the Council shall act by qualified majority.'

15. The following title shall be inserted in Part Three:

'Title IIIa

VISAS, ASYLUM, IMMIGRATION AND OTHER POLICIES RELATED TO FREE MOVEMENT OF PERSONS

Article 73i

In order to establish progressively an area of freedom, security and justice, the Council shall adopt:

(a) within a period of five years after the entry into force of the Treaty of Amsterdam, measures aimed at ensuring the free movement of persons in accordance with Article 7a, in conjunction with directly related flanking measures with respect to external border controls, asylum and immigration, in accordance with the provisions of Article 73j(2) and (3) and Article 73k(1)(a) and (2)(a), and measures to prevent and combat crime in accordance with the provisions of Article K.3(e) of the Treaty on European Union;

(b) other measures in the fields of asylum, immigration and safeguarding the rights of nationals of third countries, in accordance with the provisions of Article 73k;

(c) measures in the field of judicial cooperation in civil matters as provided for in Article 73m;

(d) appropriate measures to encourage and strengthen administrative cooperation, as provided for in Article 73n;

(e) measures in the field of police and judicial cooperation in criminal matters aimed at a high level of security by preventing and combating crime within the Union in accordance with the provisions of the Treaty on European Union.

Article 73j

The Council, acting in accordance with the procedure referred to in Article 73o, shall, within a period of five years after the entry into force of the Treaty of Amsterdam, adopt:

(1) measures with a view to ensuring, in compliance with Article 7a, the absence of any controls on persons, be they citizens of the Union or nationals of third countries, when crossing internal borders;

(2) measures on the crossing of the external borders of the Member States which shall establish:

    (a) standards and procedures to be followed by Member States in carrying out checks on persons at such borders;

    (b) rules on visas for intended stays of no more than three months, including:

        (i) the list of third countries whose nationals must be in possession of visas when crossing the external borders and those whose nationals are exempt from that requirement;

(ii) the procedures and conditions for issuing visas by Member States;

(iii) a uniform format for visas;

(iv) rules on a uniform visa;

(3) measures setting out the conditions under which nationals of third countries shall have the freedom to travel within the territory of the Member States during a period of no more than three months.

Article 73k

The Council, acting in accordance with the procedure referred to in Article 73o, shall, within a period of five years after the entry into force of the Treaty of Amsterdam, adopt:

(1) measures on asylum, in accordance with the Geneva Convention of 28 July 1951 and the Protocol of 31 January 1967 relating to the status of refugees and other relevant treaties, within the following areas:

(a) criteria and mechanisms for determining which Member State is responsible for considering an application for asylum submitted by a national of a third country in one of the Member States,

(b) minimum standards on the reception of asylum seekers in Member States,

(c) minimum standards with respect to the qualification of nationals of third countries as refugees,

(d) minimum standards on procedures in Member States for granting or withdrawing refugee status;

(2) measures on refugees and displaced persons within the following areas:

(a) minimum standards for giving temporary protection to displaced persons from third countries who cannot return to their country of origin and for persons who otherwise need international protection,

(b) promoting a balance of effort between Member States in receiving and bearing the consequences of receiving refugees and displaced persons;

(3) measures on immigration policy within the following areas:

(a) conditions of entry and residence, and standards on procedures for the issue by Member States of long term visas and residence permits, including those for the purpose of family reunion,

(b) illegal immigration and illegal residence, including repatriation of illegal residents;

(4) measures defining the rights and conditions under which nationals of third countries who are legally resident in a Member State may reside in other Member States.

Measures adopted by the Council pursuant to points 3 and 4 shall not prevent any Member State from maintaining or introducing in the areas concerned national provisions which are compatible with this Treaty and with international agreements.

Measures to be adopted pursuant to points 2(b), 3(a) and 4 shall not be subject to the five year period referred to above.

Article 73l

1.   This Title shall not affect the exercise of the responsibilities incumbent upon Member States with regard to the maintenance of law and order and the safeguarding of internal security.

2.   In the event of one or more Member States being confronted with an emergency situation characterised by a sudden inflow of nationals of third countries and without prejudice to paragraph 1, the Council may, acting by qualified majority on a proposal from the Commission, adopt provisional measures of a duration not exceeding six months for the benefit of the Member States concerned.

Article 73m

Measures in the field of judicial cooperation in civil matters having cross-border implications, to be taken in accordance with Article 73o and insofar as necessary for the proper functioning of the internal market, shall include:

(a) improving and simplifying:

   — the system for cross-border service of judicial and extrajudicial documents;

   — cooperation in the taking of evidence;

   — the recognition and enforcement of decisions in civil and commercial cases, including decisions in extrajudicial cases;

(b) promoting the compatibility of the rules applicable in the Member States concerning the conflict of laws and of jurisdiction;

(c) eliminating obstacles to the good functioning of civil proceedings, if necessary by promoting the compatibility of the rules on civil procedure applicable in the Member States.

Article 73n

The Council, acting in accordance with the procedure referred to in Article 73o, shall take measures to ensure cooperation between the relevant departments of the administrations of the Member States in the areas covered by this Title, as well as between those departments and the Commission.

Article 73o

1.   During a transitional period of five years following the entry into force of the Treaty of Amsterdam, the Council shall act unanimously on a proposal from the Commission or on the initiative of a Member State and after consulting the European Parliament.

2.   After this period of five years:

— the Council shall act on proposals from the Commission; the Commission shall examine any request made by a Member State that it submit a proposal to the Council;

— the Council, acting unanimously after consulting the European Parliament, shall take a decision with a view to providing for all or parts of the areas covered by this Title to be governed by the procedure referred to in Article 189b and adapting the provisions relating to the powers of the Court of Justice.

3.   By derogation from paragraphs 1 and 2, measures referred to in Article 73j(2)(b) (i) and (iii) shall, from the entry into force of the Treaty of Amsterdam, be adopted by the Council acting by a qualified majority on a proposal from the Commission and after consulting the European Parliament.

4.   By derogation from paragraph 2, measures referred to in Article 73j(2)(b) (ii) and (iv) shall, after a period of five years following the entry into force of the Treaty of Amsterdam, be adopted by the Council acting in accordance with the procedure referred to in Article 189b.

Article 73p

1.   Article 177 shall apply to this Title under the following circumstances and conditions: where a question on the interpretation of this Title or on the validity or interpretation of acts of the institutions of the Community based on this Title is raised in a case pending before a court or a tribunal of a Member State against whose decisions there is no judicial remedy under national law, that court or tribunal shall, if it considers that a decision on the question is necessary to enable it to give judgment, request the Court of Justice to give a ruling thereon.

2.   In any event, the Court of Justice shall not have jurisdiction to rule on any measure or decision taken pursuant to Article 73j(1) relating to the maintenance of law and order and the safeguarding of internal security.

3.   The Council, the Commission or a Member State may request the Court of Justice to give a ruling on a question of interpretation of this Title or of acts of the institutions of the Community based on this Title. The ruling given by the Court of Justice in response to such a request shall not apply to judgments of courts or tribunals of the Member States which have become *res judicata*.

Article 73q

The application of this Title shall be subject to the provisions of the Protocol on the position of the United Kingdom and Ireland and to the Protocol on the position of Denmark and without prejudice to the Protocol on the application of certain aspects of

Article 7a of the Treaty establishing the European Community to the United Kingdom and to Ireland.'

16. In Article 75(1), the introductory part shall be replaced by the following:

'1.   For the purpose of implementing Article 74, and taking into account the distinctive features of transport, the Council shall, acting in accordance with the procedure referred to in Article 189b and after consulting the Economic and Social Committee and the Committee of the Regions, lay down:'

17. In Article 100a, paragraphs 3, 4 and 5 shall be replaced by the following paragraphs:

'3.   The Commission, in its proposals envisaged in paragraph 1 concerning health, safety, environmental protection and consumer protection, will take as a base a high level of protection, taking account in particular of any new development based on scientific facts. Within their respective powers, the European Parliament and the Council will also seek to achieve this objective.

4.   If, after the adoption by the Council or by the Commission of a harmonisation measure, a Member State deems it necessary to maintain national provisions on grounds of major needs referred to in Article 36, or relating to the protection of the environment or the working environment, it shall notify the Commission of these provisions as well as the grounds for maintaining them.

5.   Moreover, without prejudice to paragraph 4, if, after the adoption by the Council or by the Commission of a harmonisation measure, a Member State deems it necessary to introduce national provisions based on new scientific evidence relating to the protection of the environment or the working environment on grounds of a problem specific to that Member State arising after the adoption of the harmonisation measure, it shall notify the Commission of the envisaged provisions as well as the grounds for introducing them.

6.   The Commission shall, within six months of the notifications as referred to in paragraphs 4 and 5, approve or reject the national provisions involved after having verified whether or not they are a means of arbitrary discrimination or a disguised restriction on trade between Member States and whether or not they shall constitute an obstacle to the functioning of the internal market.

In the absence of a decision by the Commission within this period the national provisions referred to in paragraphs 4 and 5 shall be deemed to have been approved.

When justified by the complexity of the matter and in the absence of danger for human health, the Commission may notify the Member State concerned that the period referred to in this paragraph may be extended for a further period of up to six months.

7.   When, pursuant to paragraph 6, a Member State is authorised to maintain or introduce national provisions derogating from a harmonisation measure, the Commission shall immediately examine whether to propose an adaptation to that measure.

8.   When a Member State raises a specific problem on public health in a field which has been the subject of prior harmonisation measures, it shall bring it to the attention of the Commission which shall immediately examine whether to propose appropriate measures to the Council.

9. By way of derogation from the procedure laid down in Articles 169 and 170, the Commission and any Member State may bring the matter directly before the Court of Justice if it considers that another Member State is making improper use of the powers provided for in this Article.

10. The harmonisation measures referred to above shall, in appropriate cases, include a safeguard clause authorising the Member States to take, for one or more of the non-economic reasons referred to in Article 36, provisional measures subject to a Community control procedure.'

18. Articles 100c and 100d shall be repealed.

19. The following Title shall be inserted after Title VI:

'Title VIa

EMPLOYMENT

Article 109n

Member States and the Community shall, in accordance with this Title, work towards developing a coordinated strategy for employment and particularly for promoting a skilled, trained and adaptable workforce and labour markets responsive to economic change with a view to achieving the objectives defined in Article B of the Treaty on European Union and in Article 2 of this Treaty.

Article 109o

1. Member States, through their employment policies, shall contribute to the achievement of the objectives referred to in Article 109n in a way consistent with the broad guidelines of the economic policies of the Member States and of the Community adopted pursuant to Article 103(2).

2. Member States, having regard to national practices related to the responsibilities of management and labour, shall regard promoting employment as a matter of common concern and shall coordinate their action in this respect within the Council, in accordance with the provisions of Article 109q.

Article 109p

1. The Community shall contribute to a high level of employment by encouraging cooperation between Member States and by supporting and, if necessary, complementing their action. In doing so, the competences of the Member States shall be respected.

2. The objective of a high level of employment shall be taken into consideration in the formulation and implementation of Community policies and activities.

Article 109q

1.   The European Council shall each year consider the employment situation in the Community and adopt conclusions thereon, on the basis of a joint annual report by the Council and the Commission.

2.   On the basis of the conclusions of the European Council, the Council, acting by a qualified majority on a proposal from the Commission and after consulting the European Parliament, the Economic and Social Committee, the Committee of the Regions and the Employment Committee referred to in Article 109s, shall each year draw up guidelines which the Member States shall take into account in their employment policies. These guidelines shall be consistent with the broad guidelines adopted pursuant to Article 103(2).

3.   Each Member State shall provide the Council and the Commission with an annual report on the principal measures taken to implement its employment policy in the light of the guidelines for employment as referred to in paragraph 2.

4.   The Council, on the basis of the reports referred to in paragraph 3 and having received the views of the Employment Committee, shall each year carry out an examination of the implementation of the employment policies of the Member States in the light of the guidelines for employment. The Council, acting by a qualified majority on a recommendation from the Commission, may, if it considers it appropriate in the light of that examination, make recommendations to Member States.

5.   On the basis of the results of that examination, the Council and the Commission shall make a joint annual report to the European Council on the employment situation in the Community and on the implementation of the guidelines for employment.

Article 109r

The Council, acting in accordance with the procedure referred to in Article 189b and after consulting the Economic and Social Committee and the Committee of the Regions, may adopt incentive measures designed to encourage cooperation between Member States and to support their action in the field of employment through initiatives aimed at developing exchanges of information and best practices, providing comparative analysis and advice as well as promoting innovative approaches and evaluating experiences, in particular by recourse to pilot projects.

Those measures shall not include harmonisation of the laws and regulations of the Member States.

Article 109s

The Council, after consulting the European Parliament, shall establish an Employment Committee with advisory status to promote coordination between Member States on employment and labour market policies. The tasks of the Committee shall be:

— to monitor the employment situation and employment policies in the Member States and the Community;

— without prejudice to Article 151, to formulate opinions at the request of either the Council or the Commission or on its own initiative, and to contribute to the preparation of the Council proceedings referred to in Article 109q.

In fulfilling its mandate, the Committee shall consult management and labour.

Each Member State and the Commission shall appoint two members of the Committee.'

20. In Article 113, the following paragraph shall be added:

'5.   The Council, acting unanimously on a proposal from the Commission and after consulting the European Parliament, may extend the application of paragraphs 1 to 4 to international negotiations and agreements on services and intellectual property insofar as they are not covered by these paragraphs.'

21. The following Title shall be inserted after Title VII:

'Title VIIa

CUSTOMS COOPERATION

Article 116

Within the scope of application of this Treaty, the Council, acting in accordance with the procedure referred to in Article 189b, shall take measures in order to strengthen customs cooperation between Member States and between the latter and the Commission. These measures shall not concern the application of national criminal law or the national administration of justice.'

22. Articles 117 to 120 shall be replaced by the following Articles:

'*Article 117*

The Community and the Member States, having in mind fundamental social rights such as those set out in the European Social Charter signed at Turin on 18 October 1961 and in the 1989 Community Charter of the Fundamental Social Rights of Workers, shall have as their objectives the promotion of employment, improved living and working conditions, so as to make possible their harmonisation while the improvement is being maintained, proper social protection, dialogue between management and labour, the development of human resources with a view to lasting high employment and the combating of exclusion.

To this end the Community and the Member States shall implement measures which take account of the diverse forms of national practices, in particular in the field of contractual relations, and the need to maintain the competitiveness of the Community economy.

They believe that such a development will ensue not only from the functioning of the common market, which will favour the harmonisation of social systems, but also from the procedures provided for in this Treaty and from the approximation of provisions laid down by law, regulation or administrative action.

Article 118

1.   With a view to achieving the objectives of Article 117, the Community shall support and complement the activities of the Member States in the following fields:

— improvement in particular of the working environment to protect workers' health and safety;

— working conditions;

— the information and consultation of workers;

— the integration of persons excluded from the labour market, without prejudice to Article 127;

— equality between men and women with regard to labour market opportunities and treatment at work.

2.   To this end, the Council may adopt, by means of directives, minimum requirements for gradual implementation, having regard to the conditions and technical rules obtaining in each of the Member States. Such directives shall avoid imposing administrative, financial and legal constraints in a way which would hold back the creation and development of small and medium-sized undertakings.

The Council shall act in accordance with the procedure referred to in Article 189b after consulting the Economic and Social Committee and the Committee of the Regions.

The Council, acting in accordance with the same procedure, may adopt measures designed to encourage cooperation between Member States through initiatives aimed at improving knowledge, developing exchanges of information and best practices, promoting innovative approaches and evaluating experiences in order to combat social exclusion.

3.   However, the Council shall act unanimously on a proposal from the Commission, after consulting the European Parliament, the Economic and Social Committee and the Committee of the Regions in the following areas:

— social security and social protection of workers;

— protection of workers where their employment contract is terminated;

— representation and collective defence of the interests of workers and employers, including co-determination, subject to paragraph 6;

— conditions of employment for third-country nationals legally residing in Community territory;

— financial contributions for promotion of employment and job-creation, without prejudice to the provisions relating to the Social Fund.

4.   A Member State may entrust management and labour, at their joint request, with the implementation of directives adopted pursuant to paragraphs 2 and 3.

In this case, it shall ensure that, no later than the date on which a directive must be transposed in accordance with Article 189, management and labour have introduced the necessary measures by agreement, the Member State concerned being required to take any necessary measure enabling it at any time to be in a position to guarantee the results imposed by that directive.

5. The provisions adopted pursuant to this Article shall not prevent any Member State from maintaining or introducing more stringent protective measures compatible with this Treaty.

6. The provisions of this Article shall not apply to pay, the right of association, the right to strike or the right to impose lock-outs.

Article 118a

1. The Commission shall have the task of promoting the consultation of management and labour at Community level and shall take any relevant measure to facilitate their dialogue by ensuring balanced support for the parties.

2. To this end, before submitting proposals in the social policy field, the Commission shall consult management and labour on the possible direction of Community action.

3. If, after such consultation, the Commission considers Community action advisable, it shall consult management and labour on the content of the envisaged proposal. Management and labour shall forward to the Commission an opinion or, where appropriate, a recommendation.

4. On the occasion of such consultation, management and labour may inform the Commission of their wish to initiate the process provided for in Article 118b. The duration of the procedure shall not exceed nine months, unless the management and labour concerned and the Commission decide jointly to extend it.

Article 118b

1. Should management and labour so desire, the dialogue between them at Community level may lead to contractual relations, including agreements.

2. Agreements concluded at Community level shall be implemented either in accordance with the procedures and practices specific to management and labour and the Member States or, in matters covered by Article 118, at the joint request of the signatory parties, by a Council decision on a proposal from the Commission.

The Council shall act by qualified majority, except where the agreement in question contains one or more provisions relating to one of the areas referred to in Article 118(3), in which case it shall act unanimously.

Article 118c

With a view to achieving the objectives of Article 117 and without prejudice to the other provisions of this Treaty, the Commission shall encourage cooperation between the Member States and facilitate the coordination of their action in all social policy fields under this chapter, particularly in matters relating to:

— employment;

— labour law and working conditions;

— basic and advanced vocational training;

— social security;

— prevention of occupational accidents and diseases;

— occupational hygiene;

— the right of association and collective bargaining between employers and workers.

To this end, the Commission shall act in close contact with Member States by making studies, delivering opinions and arranging consultations both on problems arising at national level and on those of concern to international organisations.

Before delivering the opinions provided for in this Article, the Commission shall consult the Economic and Social Committee.

Article 119

1.   Each Member State shall ensure that the principle of equal pay for male and female workers for equal work or work of equal value is applied.

2.   For the purpose of this Article, "pay" means the ordinary basic or minimum wage or salary and any other consideration, whether in cash or in kind, which the worker receives directly or indirectly, in respect of his employment, from his employer.

Equal pay without discrimination based on sex means:

(a) that pay for the same work at piece rates shall be calculated on the basis of the same unit of measurement;

(b) that pay for work at time rates shall be the same for the same job.

3.   The Council, acting in accordance with the procedure referred to in Article 189b, and after consulting the Economic and Social Committee, shall adopt measures to ensure the application of the principle of equal opportunities and equal treatment of men and women in matters of employment and occupation, including the principle of equal pay for equal work or work of equal value.

4.   With a view to ensuring full equality in practice between men and women in working life, the principle of equal treatment shall not prevent any Member State from maintaining or adopting measures providing for specific advantages in order to make it easier for the under-represented sex to pursue a vocational activity or to prevent or compensate for disadvantages in professional careers.

Article 119a

Member States shall endeavour to maintain the existing equivalence between paid holiday schemes.

Article 120

The Commission shall draw up a report each year on progress in achieving the objectives of Article 117, including the demographic situation in the Community. It shall forward the report to the European Parliament, the Council and the Economic and Social Committee.

The European Parliament may invite the Commission to draw up reports on particular problems concerning the social situation.'

23. Article 125 shall be replaced by the following:

'*Article 125*

The Council, acting in accordance with the procedure referred to in Article 189b and after consulting the Economic and Social Committee and the Committee of the Regions, shall adopt implementing decisions relating to the European Social Fund.'

24. Article 127(4) shall be replaced by the following:

'4. The Council, acting in accordance with the procedure referred to in Article 189b and after consulting the Economic and Social Committee and the Committee of the Regions, shall adopt measures to contribute to the achievement of the objectives referred to in this Article, excluding any harmonisation of the laws and regulations of the Member States.'

25. Article 128(4) shall be replaced by the following:

'4. The Community shall take cultural aspects into account in its action under other provisions of this Treaty, in particular in order to respect and to promote the diversity of its cultures.'

26. Article 129 shall be replaced by the following:

'*Article 129*

1. A high level of human health protection shall be ensured in the definition and implementation of all Community policies and activities.

Community action, which shall complement national policies, shall be directed towards improving public health, preventing human illness and diseases, and obviating sources of danger to human health. Such action shall cover the fight against the major health scourges, by promoting research into their causes, their transmission and their prevention, as well as health information and education.

The Community shall complement the Member States' action in reducing drugs-related health damage, including information and prevention.

2. The Community shall encourage cooperation between the Member States in the areas referred to in this Article and, if necessary, lend support to their action.

Member States shall, in liaison with the Commission, coordinate among themselves their policies and programmes in the areas referred to in paragraph 1. The Commission may, in close contact with the Member States, take any useful initiative to promote such co-ordination.

3.   The Community and the Member States shall foster cooperation with third countries and the competent international organisations in the sphere of public health.

4.   The Council, acting in accordance with the procedure referred to in Article 189b and after consulting the Economic and Social Committee and the Committee of the Regions, shall contribute to the achievement of the objectives referred to in this Article through adopting:

(a) measures setting high standards of quality and safety of organs and substances of human origin, blood and blood derivatives; these measures shall not prevent any Member State from maintaining or introducing more stringent protective measures;

(b) by way of derogation from Article 43, measures in the veterinary and phytosanitary fields which have as their direct objective the protection of public health;

(c) incentive measures designed to protect and improve human health, excluding any harmonisation of the laws and regulations of the Member States.

The Council, acting by a qualified majority on a proposal from the Commission, may also adopt recommendations for the purposes set out in this Article.

5.   Community action in the field of public health shall fully respect the responsibilities of the Member States for the organisation and delivery of health services and medical care. In particular, measures referred to in paragraph 4(a) shall not affect national provisions on the donation or medical use of organs and blood.'

27. Article 129a shall be replaced by the following:

'*Article 129a*

1.   In order to promote the interests of consumers and to ensure a high level of consumer protection, the Community shall contribute to protecting the health, safety and economic interests of consumers, as well as to promoting their right to information, education and to organise themselves in order to safeguard their interests.

2.   Consumer protection requirements shall be taken into account in defining and implementing other Community policies and activities.

3.   The Community shall contribute to the attainment of the objectives referred to in paragraph 1 through:

(a) measures adopted pursuant to Article 100a in the context of the completion of the internal market;

(b) measures which support, supplement and monitor the policy pursued by the Member States.

4.   The Council, acting in accordance with the procedure referred to in Article 189b and after consulting the Economic and Social Committee, shall adopt the measures referred to in paragraph 3(b).

5.   Measures adopted pursuant to paragraph 4 shall not prevent any Member State from maintaining or introducing more stringent protective measures. Such measures must be compatible with this Treaty. The Commission shall be notified of them.'

28. In the first subparagraph of Article 129c(1), the first part of the third indent shall be replaced by the following:

'— may support projects of common interest supported by Member States, which are identified in the framework of the guidelines referred to in the first indent, particularly through feasibility studies, loan guarantees or interest-rate subsidies;'.

29. Article 129d shall be amended as follows:

(a) the first paragraph shall be replaced by the following:

'The guidelines and other measures referred to in Article 129c(1) shall be adopted by the Council, acting in accordance with the procedure referred to in Article 189b and after consulting the Economic and Social Committee and the Committee of the Regions.';

(b) the third paragraph shall be deleted.

30. In Article 130a, the second paragraph shall be replaced by the following:

'In particular, the Community shall aim at reducing disparities between the levels of development of the various regions and the backwardness of the least favoured regions or islands, including rural areas.'

31. In Article 130e, the first paragraph shall be replaced by the following:

'Implementing decisions relating to the European Regional Development Fund shall be taken by the Council, acting in accordance with the procedure referred to in Article 189b and after consulting the Economic and Social Committee and the Committee of the Regions.'

32. In Article 130i(1), the first subparagraph shall be replaced by the following:

'1.   A multi-annual framework programme, setting out all the activities of the Community, shall be adopted by the Council, acting in accordance with the procedure referred to in Article 189b after consulting the Economic and Social Committee.'

33. Article 130o shall be replaced by the following:

'*Article 130o*

The Council, acting by qualified majority on a proposal from the Commission and after consulting the European Parliament and the Economic and Social Committee, shall adopt the provisions referred to in Article 130n.

The Council, acting in accordance with the procedure referred to in Article 189b and after consulting the Economic and Social Committee, shall adopt the provisions referred to in Articles 130j, 130k and 130l. Adoption of the supplementary programmes shall require the agreement of the Member States concerned.'

34. Article 130r(2) shall be replaced by the following:

'2.   Community policy on the environment shall aim at a high level of protection taking into account the diversity of situations in the various regions of the Community. It shall be based on the precautionary principle and on the principles that preventive action should be taken, that environmental damage should as a priority be rectified at source and that the polluter should pay.

In this context, harmonisation measures answering environmental protection requirements shall include, where appropriate, a safeguard clause allowing Member States to take provisional measures, for non-economic environmental reasons, subject to a Community inspection procedure.'

35. Article 130s shall be amended as follows:

(a) Paragraph 1 shall be replaced by the following:

'1.   The Council, acting in accordance with the procedure referred to in Article 189b and after consulting the Economic and Social Committee and the Committee of the Regions, shall decide what action is to be taken by the Community in order to achieve the objectives referred to in Article 130r.';

(b) The introductory part of paragraph 2 shall be replaced by the following:

'2.   By way of derogation from the decision making procedure provided for in paragraph 1 and without prejudice to Article 100a, the Council, acting unanimously on a proposal from the Commission and after consulting the European Parliament, the Economic and Social Committee and the Committee of the Regions, shall adopt:';

(c) The first subparagraph of paragraph 3 shall be replaced by the following:

'3.   In other areas, general action programmes setting out priority objectives to be attained shall be adopted by the Council, acting in accordance with the procedure referred to in Article 189b and after consulting the Economic and Social Committee and the Committee of the Regions.'

36. Article 130w(1) shall be replaced by the following:

'1.   Without prejudice to the other provisions of this Treaty, the Council, acting in accordance with the procedure referred to in Article 189b, shall adopt the measures necessary to further the objectives referred to in Article 130u. Such measures may take the form of multi-annual programmes.'

37. In Article 137, the following paragraph shall be added:

'The number of Members of the European Parliament shall not exceed seven hundred.'

38. Article 138 shall be amended as follows:

(a) in paragraph 3, the first subparagraph shall be replaced by the following:

'3.   The European Parliament shall draw up a proposal for elections by direct universal suffrage in accordance with a uniform procedure in all Member States or in accordance with principles common to all Member States.';

(b) the following paragraph shall be added:

'4.   The European Parliament shall, after seeking an opinion from the Commission and with the approval of the Council acting unanimously, lay down the regulations and general conditions governing the performance of the duties of its Members.'

39. Article 151 shall be replaced by the following:

'*Article 151*

1.   A committee consisting of the Permanent Representatives of the Member States shall be responsible for preparing the work of the Council and for carrying out the tasks assigned to it by the Council. The Committee may adopt procedural decisions in cases provided for in the Council's Rules of Procedure.

2.   The Council shall be assisted by a General Secretariat, under the responsibility of a Secretary-General, High Representative for the common foreign and security policy, who shall be assisted by a Deputy Secretary-General responsible for the running of the General Secretariat. The Secretary-General and the Deputy Secretary-General shall be appointed by the Council acting unanimously.

The Council shall decide on the organisation of the General Secretariat.

3.   The Council shall adopt its Rules of Procedure.

For the purpose of applying Article 191a(3), the Council shall elaborate in these Rules the conditions under which the public shall have access to Council documents. For the purpose of this paragraph, the Council shall define the cases in which it is to be regarded as acting in its legislative capacity, with a view to allowing greater access to documents in those cases, while at the same time preserving the effectiveness of its decision making process. In any event, when the Council acts in its legislative capacity, the results of votes and explanations of vote as well as statements in the minutes shall be made public.'

40. In Article 158(2), the first and second subparagraphs shall be replaced by the following:

'2.   The governments of the Member States shall nominate by common accord the person they intend to appoint as President of the Commission; the nomination shall be approved by the European Parliament.

The governments of the Member States shall, by common accord with the nominee for President, nominate the other persons whom they intend to appoint as Members of the Commission.'

41. In Article 163, the following paragraph shall be inserted as the first paragraph:

'The Commission shall work under the political guidance of its President.'

42. In Article 173, the third paragraph shall be replaced by the following:

'The Court of Justice shall have jurisdiction under the same conditions in actions brought by the European Parliament, by the Court of Auditors and by the ECB for the purpose of protecting their prerogatives.'

43. Article 188c shall be amended as follows:

(a) The second subparagraph of paragraph 1 shall be replaced by the following:

'The Court of Auditors shall provide the European Parliament and the Council with a statement of assurance as to the reliability of the accounts and the legality and regularity of the underlying transactions which shall be published in the *Official Journal of the European Communities*.';

(b) The first subparagraph of paragraph 2 shall be replaced by the following:

'2.   The Court of Auditors shall examine whether all revenue has been received and all expenditure incurred in a lawful and regular manner and whether the financial management has been sound. In doing so, it shall report in particular on any cases of irregularity.';

(c) Paragraph 3 shall be replaced by the following:

'3.   The audit shall be based on records and, if necessary, performed on the spot in the other institutions of the Community, on the premises of any body which manages revenue or expenditure on behalf of the Community and in the Member States, including on the premises of any natural or legal person in receipt of payments from the budget. In the Member States the audit shall be carried out in liaison with national audit bodies or, if these do not have the necessary powers, with the competent national departments. The Court of Auditors and the national audit bodies of the Member States shall cooperate in a spirit of trust while maintaining their independence. These bodies or departments shall inform the Court of Auditors whether they intend to take part in the audit.

The other institutions of the Community, any bodies managing revenue or expenditure on behalf of the Community, any natural or legal person in receipt of payments from the budget, and the national audit bodies or, if these do not have the necessary powers, the competent national departments, shall forward to the Court of Auditors, at its request, any document or information necessary to carry out its task.

In respect of the European Investment Bank's activity in managing Community expenditure and revenue, the Court's rights of access to information held by the Bank shall be governed by an agreement between the Court, the Bank and the Commission. In the absence of an agreement, the Court shall nevertheless have access to information necessary for the audit of Community expenditure and revenue managed by the Bank.'

44. Article 189b shall be replaced by the following:

'*Article 189b*

1. Where reference is made in this Treaty to this Article for the adoption of an act, the following procedure shall apply.

2. The Commission shall submit a proposal to the European Parliament and the Council.

The Council, acting by a qualified majority after obtaining the opinion of the European Parliament,

— if it approves all the amendments contained in the European Parliament's opinion, may adopt the proposed act thus amended;

— if the European Parliament does not propose any amendments, may adopt the proposed act;

— shall otherwise adopt a common position and communicate it to the European Parliament. The Council shall inform the European Parliament fully of the reasons which led it to adopt its common position. The Commission shall inform the European Parliament fully of its position.

If, within three months of such communication, the European Parliament:

(a) approves the common position or has not taken a decision, the act in question shall be deemed to have been adopted in accordance with that common position;

(b) rejects, by an absolute majority of its component members, the common position, the proposed act shall be deemed not to have been adopted;

(c) proposes amendments to the common position by an absolute majority of its component members, the amended text shall be forwarded to the Council and to the Commission, which shall deliver an opinion on those amendments.

3. If, within three months of the matter being referred to it, the Council, acting by a qualified majority, approves all the amendments of the European Parliament, the act in question shall be deemed to have been adopted in the form of the common position thus

amended; however, the Council shall act unanimously on the amendments on which the Commission has delivered a negative opinion. If the Council does not approve all the amendments, the President of the Council, in agreement with the President of the European Parliament, shall within six weeks convene a meeting of the Conciliation Committee.

4.   The Conciliation Committee, which shall be composed of the members of the Council or their representatives and an equal number of representatives of the European Parliament, shall have the task of reaching agreement on a joint text, by a qualified majority of the members of the Council or their representatives and by a majority of the representatives of the European Parliament. The Commission shall take part in the Conciliation Committee's proceedings and shall take all the necessary initiatives with a view to reconciling the positions of the European Parliament and the Council. In fulfilling this task, the Conciliation Committee shall address the common position on the basis of the amendments proposed by the European Parliament.

5.   If, within six weeks of its being convened, the Conciliation Committee approves a joint text, the European Parliament, acting by an absolute majority of the votes cast, and the Council, acting by a qualified majority, shall each have a period of six weeks from that approval in which to adopt the act in question in accordance with the joint text. If either of the two institutions fails to approve the proposed act within that period, it shall be deemed not to have been adopted.

6.   Where the Conciliation Committee does not approve a joint text, the proposed act shall be deemed not to have been adopted.

7.   The periods of three months and six weeks referred to in this Article shall be extended by a maximum of one month and two weeks respectively at the initiative of the European Parliament or the Council.'

45. The following Article shall be inserted:

'*Article 191a*

1.   Any citizen of the Union, and any natural or legal person residing or having their registered office in a Member State, shall have a right of access to European Parliament, Council and Commission documents, subject to the principles and the conditions to be defined in accordance with paragraphs 2 and 3.

2.   General principles and limits on grounds of public or private interest governing this right of access to documents shall be determined by the Council, acting in accordance with the procedure referred to in Article 189b within two years of the entry into force of the Treaty of Amsterdam.

3.   Each institution referred to above shall elaborate in its own Rules of Procedure specific provisions regarding access to its documents.'

46. In Article 198, the following paragraph shall be added:

'The Committee may be consulted by the European Parliament.'

47. In Article 198a, the third paragraph shall be replaced by the following:

'The members of the Committee and an equal number of alternate members shall be appointed for four years by the Council acting unanimously on proposals from the respective Member States. Their term of office shall be renewable. No member of the Committee shall at the same time be a Member of the European Parliament.'

48. In Article 198b the second paragraph shall be replaced by the following:

'It shall adopt its Rules of Procedure.'

49. Article 198c shall be amended as follows:

(a) the first paragraph shall be replaced by the following:

'The Committee of the Regions shall be consulted by the Council or by the Commission where this Treaty so provides and in all other cases, in particular those which concern cross-border cooperation, in which one of these two institutions considers it appropriate.';

(b) after the third paragraph, the following paragraph shall be inserted:

'The Committee of the Regions may be consulted by the European Parliament.'

50. In Article 205, the first paragraph shall be replaced by the following:

'The Commission shall implement the budget, in accordance with the provisions of the regulations made pursuant to Article 209, on its own responsibility and within the limits of the appropriations, having regard to the principles of sound financial management. Member States shall cooperate with the Commission to ensure that the appropriations are used in accordance with the principles of sound financial management.'

51. Article 206(1) shall be replaced by the following:

'1.   The European Parliament, acting on a recommendation from the Council which shall act by a qualified majority, shall give a discharge to the Commission in respect of the implementation of the budget. To this end, the Council and the European Parliament in turn shall examine the accounts and the financial statement referred to in Article 205a, the annual report by the Court of Auditors together with the replies of the institutions under audit to the observations of the Court of Auditors, the statement of assurance referred to in Article 188c(1), second subparagraph and any relevant special reports by the Court of Auditors.'

52. Article 209a shall be replaced by the following:

'*Article 209a*

1.   The Community and the Member States shall counter fraud and any other illegal activities affecting the financial interests of the Community through measures to be taken in accordance with this Article, which shall act as a deterrent and be such as to afford effective protection in the Member States.

2.   Member States shall take the same measures to counter fraud affecting the financial interests of the Community as they take to counter fraud affecting their own financial interests.

3.   Without prejudice to other provisions of this Treaty, the Member States shall co-ordinate their action aimed at protecting the financial interests of the Community against fraud. To this end they shall organise, together with the Commission, close and regular cooperation between the competent authorities.

4.   The Council, acting in accordance with the procedure referred to in Article 189b, after consulting the Court of Auditors, shall adopt the necessary measures in the fields of the prevention of and fight against fraud affecting the financial interests of the Community with a view to affording effective and equivalent protection in the Member States. These measures shall not concern the application of national criminal law or the national administration of justice.

5.   The Commission, in cooperation with Member States, shall each year submit to the European Parliament and to the Council a report on the measures taken for the implementation of this Article.'

53. The following Article shall be inserted:

'*Article 213a*

1.   Without prejudice to Article 5 of the Protocol on the Statute of the European System of Central Banks and of the European Central Bank, the Council, acting in accordance with the procedure referred to in Article 189b, shall adopt measures for the production of statistics where necessary for the performance of the activities of the Community.

2.   The production of Community statistics shall conform to impartiality, reliability, objectivity, scientific independence, cost-effectiveness and statistical confidentiality; it shall not entail excessive burdens on economic operators.'

54. The following Article shall be inserted:

'*Article 213b*

1.   From 1 January 1999, Community acts on the protection of individuals with regard to the processing of personal data and the free movement of such data shall apply to the institutions and bodies set up by, or on the basis of, this Treaty.

2.   Before the date referred to in paragraph 1, the Council, acting in accordance with the procedure referred to in Article 189b, shall establish an independent supervisory body responsible for monitoring the application of such Community acts to Community institutions and bodies and shall adopt any other relevant provisions as appropriate.'

55. Article 227(2) shall be replaced by the following:

'2.   The provisions of this Treaty shall apply to the French overseas departments, the Azores, Madeira and the Canary Islands.

However, taking account of the structural social and economic situation of the French overseas departments, the Azores, Madeira and the Canary Islands, which is compounded by their remoteness, insularity, small size, difficult topography and climate, economic dependence on a few products, the permanence and combination of which severely restrain their development, the Council, acting by a qualified majority on a proposal from the Commission and after consulting the European Parliament, shall adopt specific measures aimed, in particular, at laying down the conditions of application of the present Treaty to those regions, including common policies.

The Council shall, when adopting the relevant measures referred to in the second subparagraph, take into account areas such as customs and trade policies, fiscal policy, free zones, agriculture and fisheries policies, conditions for supply of raw materials and essential consumer goods, State aids and conditions of access to structural funds and to horizontal Community programmes.

The Council shall adopt the measures referred to in the second subparagraph taking into account the special characteristics and constraints of the outermost regions without under-mining the integrity and the coherence of the Community legal order, including the internal market and common policies.'

56. Article 228 shall be amended as follows:

(a) the second subparagraph of paragraph 1 shall be replaced by the following:

'In exercising the powers conferred upon it by this paragraph, the Council shall act by a qualified majority, except in the cases where the first subparagraph of paragraph 2 provides that the Council shall act unanimously.';

(b) paragraph 2 shall be replaced by the following:

'2.   Subject to the powers vested in the Commission in this field, the signing, which may be accompanied by a decision on provisional application before entry into force, and the conclusion of the agreements shall be decided on by the Council, acting by a qualified majority on a proposal from the Commission. The Council shall act unani-mously when the agreement covers a field for which unanimity is required for the adoption of internal rules and for the agreements referred to in Article 238.

By way of derogation from the rules laid down in paragraph 3, the same procedures shall apply for a decision to suspend the application of an agreement, and for the purpose of establishing the positions to be adopted on behalf of the Community in a body set up by an agreement based on Article 238, when that body is called upon to adopt decisions having legal effects, with the exception of decisions supplementing or amending the institutional framework of the agreement.

The European Parliament shall be immediately and fully informed on any decision under this paragraph concerning the provisional application or the suspension of agreements, or the establishment of the Community position in a body set up by an agreement based on Article 238.'

57. The following Article shall be inserted:

'*Article 236*

1.   Where a decision has been taken to suspend the voting rights of the representative of the government of a Member State in accordance with Article F.1(2) of the Treaty on European Union, these voting rights shall also be suspended with regard to this Treaty.

2.   Moreover, where the existence of a serious and persistent breach by a Member State of principles mentioned in Article F(1) of the Treaty on European Union has been determined in accordance with Article F.1(1) of that Treaty, the Council, acting by a qualified majority, may decide to suspend certain of the rights deriving from the application of this Treaty to the Member State in question. In doing so, the Council shall take into account the possible consequences of such a suspension on the rights and obligations of natural and legal persons.

The obligations of the Member State in question under this Treaty shall in any case continue to be binding on that State.

3.   The Council, acting by a qualified majority, may decide subsequently to vary or revoke measures taken in accordance with paragraph 2 in response to changes in the situation which led to their being imposed.

4.   When taking decisions referred to in paragraphs 2 and 3, the Council shall act without taking into account the votes of the representative of the government of the Member State in question. By way of derogation from Article 148(2) a qualified majority shall be defined as the same proportion of the weighted votes of the members of the Council concerned as laid down in Article 148(2).

This paragraph shall also apply in the event of voting rights being suspended in accordance with paragraph 1. In such cases, a decision requiring unanimity shall be taken without the vote of the representative of the government of the Member State in question.'

58. The Protocol on Social Policy and the Agreement on social policy attached thereto shall be repealed.

59. The Protocol on the Economic and Social Committee and the Committee of the Regions shall be repealed.

Article 3

The Treaty establishing the European Coal and Steel Community shall be amended in accordance with the provisions of this Article.

1. In Article 10(2) the first and second subparagraphs shall be replaced by the following:

'2.   The governments of the Member States shall nominate by common accord the person they intend to appoint as President of the Commission; the nomination shall be approved by the European Parliament.

The governments of the Member States shall, by common accord with the nominee for President, nominate the other persons whom they intend to appoint as Members of the Commission.'

2. In Article 13, the following paragraph shall be inserted as the first paragraph:

'The Commission shall work under the political guidance of its President.'

3. In Article 20, the following paragraph shall be added:

'The number of Members of the European Parliament shall not exceed seven hundred.'

4. Article 21 shall be amended as follows:

(a) in paragraph 3, the first subparagraph shall be replaced by the following:

'3. The European Parliament shall draw up a proposal for elections by direct universal suffrage in accordance with a uniform procedure in all Member States or in accordance with principles common to all Member States.';

(b) the following paragraph shall be added:

'4. The European Parliament shall, after seeking an opinion from the Commission and with the approval of the Council acting unanimously, lay down the regulations and general conditions governing the performance of the duties of its Members.'

5. Article 30 shall be replaced by the following:

'*Article 30*

1. A committee consisting of the Permanent Representatives of the Member States shall be responsible for preparing the work of the Council and for carrying out the tasks assigned to it by the Council. The Committee may adopt procedural decisions in cases provided for in the Council's Rules of Procedure.

2. The Council shall be assisted by a General Secretariat, under the responsibility of a Secretary-General, High Representative for the common foreign and security policy, who shall be assisted by a Deputy Secretary-General responsible for the running of the General Secretariat. The Secretary-General and the Deputy Secretary-General shall be appointed by the Council acting unanimously.

The Council shall decide on the organisation of the General Secretariat.

3. The Council shall adopt its Rules of Procedure.'

6. In Article 33, the fourth paragraph shall be replaced by the following:

'The Court of Justice shall have jurisdiction under the same conditions in actions brought by the European Parliament and by the Court of Auditors for the purpose of protecting their prerogatives.'

7. Article 45c shall be amended as follows:

(a) The second subparagraph of paragraph 1 shall be replaced by the following:

'The Court of Auditors shall provide the European Parliament and the Council with a statement of assurance as to the reliability of the accounts and the legality and regularity of the underlying transactions which shall be published in the *Official Journal of the European Communities*.';

(b) The first subparagraph of paragraph 2 shall be replaced by the following:

'2. The Court of Auditors shall examine whether all revenue has been received and all expenditure incurred in a lawful and regular manner and whether the financial management has been sound. In doing so, it shall report in particular on any cases of irregularity.';

(c) Paragraph 3 shall be replaced by the following:

'3. The audit shall be based on records and, if necessary, performed on the spot in the other institutions of the Community, on the premises of any body which manages revenue or expenditure on behalf of the Community and in the Member States, including on the premises of any natural or legal person in receipt of payments from the budget. In the Member States the audit shall be carried out in liaison with national audit bodies or, if these do not have the necessary powers, with the competent national departments. The Court of Auditors and the national audit bodies of the Member States shall cooperate in a spirit of trust while maintaining their independence. These bodies or departments shall inform the Court of Auditors whether they intend to take part in the audit.

The other institutions of the Community, any bodies managing revenue or expenditure on behalf of the Community, any natural or legal person in receipt of payments from the budget, and the national audit bodies or, if these do not have the necessary powers, the competent national departments, shall forward to the Court of Auditors, at its request, any document or information necessary to carry out its task.

In respect of the European Investment Bank's activity in managing Community expenditure and revenue, the Court's rights of access to information held by the Bank shall be governed by an agreement between the Court, the Bank and the Commission. In the absence of an agreement, the Court shall nevertheless have access to information necessary for the audit of Community expenditure and revenue managed by the Bank.'

8. In Article 78c, the first paragraph shall be replaced by the following:

'The Commission shall implement the budget, in accordance with the provisions of the regulations made pursuant to Article 78h, on its own responsibility and within the limits of the appropriations, having regard to the principles of sound financial management. Member States shall cooperate with the Commission to ensure that the appropriations are used in accordance with the principles of sound financial management.'

9. Article 78g(1) shall be replaced by the following:

'1.   The European Parliament, acting on a recommendation from the Council which shall act by a qualified majority, shall give a discharge to the Commission in respect of the implementation of the budget. To this end, the Council and the European Parliament in turn shall examine the accounts and the financial statement referred to in Article 78d, the annual report by the Court of Auditors together with the replies of the institutions under audit to the observations of the Court of Auditors, the statement of assurance referred to in Article 45c(1), second subparagraph, and any relevant special reports by the Court of Auditors.'

10. The following Article shall be inserted:

'*Article 96*

1.   Where a decision has been taken to suspend the voting rights of the representative of the government of a Member State in accordance with Article F.1(2) of the Treaty on European Union, these voting rights shall also be suspended with regard to this Treaty.

2.   Moreover, where the existence of a serious and persistent breach by a Member State of principles mentioned in Article F(1) of the Treaty on European Union has been determined in accordance with Article F.1(1) of that Treaty, the Council, acting by a qualified majority, may decide to suspend certain of the rights deriving from the application of this Treaty to the Member State in question. In doing so, the Council shall take into account the possible consequences of such a suspension on the rights and obligations of natural and legal persons.

The obligations of the Member State in question under this Treaty shall in any case continue to be binding on that State.

3.   The Council, acting by a qualified majority, may decide subsequently to vary or revoke measures taken in accordance with paragraph 2 in response to changes in the situation which led to their being imposed.

4.   When taking decisions referred to in paragraphs 2 and 3, the Council shall act without taking into account the votes of the representative of the government of the Member State in question. By way of derogation from Article 28, fourth paragraph, a qualified majority shall be defined as the same proportion of the weighted votes of the members of the Council concerned as laid down in Article 28, fourth paragraph.

This paragraph shall also apply in the event of voting rights being suspended in accordance with paragraph 1. In such cases, a decision requiring unanimity shall be taken without the vote of the representative of the government of the Member State in question.'

Article 4

The Treaty establishing the European Atomic Energy Community shall be amended in accordance with the provisions of this Article.

1. In Article 107, the following paragraph shall be added:

'The number of Members of the European Parliament shall not exceed seven hundred.'

2. Article 108 shall be amended as follows:

(a) in paragraph 3, the first subparagraph shall be replaced by the following:

'3.   The European Parliament shall draw up a proposal for elections by direct universal suffrage in accordance with a uniform procedure in all Member States or in accordance with principles common to all Member States.';

(b) the following paragraph shall be added:

'4.   The European Parliament shall, after seeking an opinion from the Commission and with the approval of the Council acting unanimously, lay down the regulations and general conditions governing the performance of the duties of its Members.'

3. Article 121 shall be replaced by the following:

'*Article 121*

1.   A committee consisting of the Permanent Representatives of the Member States shall be responsible for preparing the work of the Council and for carrying out the tasks assigned to it by the Council. The Committee may adopt procedural decisions in cases provided for in the Council's Rules of Procedure.

2.   The Council shall be assisted by a General Secretariat, under the responsibility of a Secretary-General, High Representative for the common foreign and security policy, who shall be assisted by a Deputy Secretary-General responsible for the running of the General Secretariat. The Secretary-General and the Deputy Secretary-General shall be appointed by the Council acting unanimously.

The Council shall decide on the organisation of the General Secretariat.

3.   The Council shall adopt its Rules of Procedure.'

4. In Article 127, the first and second subparagraphs of paragraph 2 shall be replaced by the following:

'2.   The governments of the Member States shall nominate by common accord the person they intend to appoint as President of the Commission; the nomination shall be approved by the European Parliament.

The governments of the Member States shall, by common accord with the nominee for President, nominate the other persons whom they intend to appoint as Members of the Commission.'

5. In Article 132, the following paragraph shall be inserted as the first paragraph:

'The Commission shall work under the political guidance of its President.'

6. In Article 146, the third paragraph shall be replaced by the following:

'The Court of Justice shall have jurisdiction under the same conditions in actions brought by the European Parliament and by the Court of Auditors for the purpose of protecting their prerogatives,'

7. Article 160c shall be amended as follows:

(a) the second subparagraph of paragraph 1 shall be replaced by the following:

'The Court of Auditors shall provide the European Parliament and the Council with a statement of assurance as to the reliability of the accounts and the legality and regularity of the underlying transactions which shall be published in the *Official Journal of the European Communities*.';

(b) the first subparagraph of paragraph 2 shall be replaced by the following:

'2.   The Court of Auditors shall examine whether all revenue has been received and all expenditure incurred in a lawful and regular manner and whether the financial management has been sound. In doing so, it shall report in particular on any cases of irregularity.';

(c) paragraph 3 shall be replaced by the following:

'3.   The audit shall be based on records and, if necessary, performed on the spot in the other institutions of the Community, on the premises of any body which manages revenue or expenditure on behalf of the Community and in the Member States, including on the premises of any natural or legal person in receipt of payments from the budget. In the Member States the audit shall be carried out in liaison with national audit bodies or, if these do not have the necessary powers, with the competent national departments. The Court of Auditors and the national audit bodies of the Member States shall cooperate in a spirit of trust while maintaining their independence. These bodies or departments shall inform the Court of Auditors whether they intend to take part in the audit.

The other institutions of the Community, any bodies managing revenue or expenditure on behalf of the Community, any natural or legal person in receipt of payments from the budget, and the national audit bodies or, if these do not have the necessary powers, the competent national departments, shall forward to the Court of Auditors, at its request, any document or information necessary to carry out its task.

In respect of the European Investment Bank's activity in managing Community expenditure and revenue, the Court's rights of access to information held by the Bank shall be governed by an agreement between the Court, the Bank and the Commission. In the absence of an agreement, the Court shall nevertheless have access to information necessary for the audit of Community expenditure and revenue managed by the Bank.'

8. In Article 170, the following paragraph shall be added:

'The Committee may be consulted by the European Parliament.'

9. In Article 179, the first paragraph shall be replaced by the following:

'The Commission shall implement the budget, in accordance with the provisions of the regulations made pursuant to Article 183, on its own responsibility and within the limits of the appropriations, having regard to the principles of sound financial management. Member States shall cooperate with the Commission to ensure that the appropriations are used in accordance with the principles of sound financial management.'

10. Article 180b(1) shall be replaced by the following:

'1.   The European Parliament, acting on a recommendation from the Council which shall act by a qualified majority, shall give a discharge to the Commission in respect of the implementation of the budget. To this end, the Council and the European Parliament in turn shall examine the accounts and the financial statement referred to in Article 179a, the annual report by the Court of Auditors together with the replies of the institutions under audit to the observations of the Court of Auditors, the statement of assurance referred to in Article 160c(1), second subparagraph, and any relevant special reports by the Court of Auditors.'

11. The following Article shall be inserted:

'*Article 204*

1.   Where a decision has been taken to suspend the voting rights of the representative of the government of a Member State in accordance with Article F.1(2) of the Treaty on European Union, these voting rights shall also be suspended with regard to this Treaty.

2.   Moreover, where the existence of a serious and persistent breach by a Member State of principles mentioned in Article F(1) of the Treaty on European Union has been determined in accordance with Article F.1(1) of that Treaty, the Council, acting by a qualified majority, may decide to suspend certain of the rights deriving from the application of this Treaty to the Member State in question. In doing so, the Council shall take into account the possible consequences of such a suspension on the rights and obligations of natural and legal persons.

The obligations of the Member State in question under this Treaty shall in any case continue to be binding on that State.

3.   The Council, acting by a qualified majority, may decide subsequently to vary or revoke measures taken in accordance with paragraph 2 in response to changes in the situation which led to their being imposed.

4.   When taking decisions referred to in paragraphs 2 and 3, the Council shall act without taking into account the votes of the representative of the government of the Member State in question. By way of derogation from Article 118(2) a qualified majority shall be defined as the same proportion of the weighted votes of the members of the Council concerned as laid down in Article 118(2).

This paragraph shall also apply in the event of voting rights being suspended in accordance with paragraph 1. In such cases, a decision requiring unanimity shall be taken without the vote of the representative of the government of the Member State in question.'

Article 5

The Act concerning the election of the representatives of the European Parliament by direct universal suffrage annexed to the Council Decision of 20 September 1976 shall be amended in accordance with the provisions of this Article.

1. In Article 2, the following paragraph shall be added:

'In the event of amendments to this Article, the number of representatives elected in each Member State must ensure appropriate representation of the peoples of the States brought together in the Community.'.

2. In Article 6(1), the following indent shall be inserted after the fifth indent:

'— member of the Committee of the Regions,'.

3. Article 7(2) shall be replaced by the following:

'2.   Pending the entry into force of a uniform electoral procedure or a procedure based on common principles and subject to the other provisions of this Act, the electoral procedure shall be governed in each Member State by its national provisions.'

4. Article 11 shall be replaced by the following:

'Pending the entry into force of the uniform electoral procedure or the procedure based on common principles referred to in Article 7, the European Parliament shall verify the credentials of representatives. For this purpose it shall take note of the results declared officially by the Member States and shall rule on any disputes which may arise out of the provisions of this Act other than those arising out of the national provisions to which the Act refers.'

5. Article 12(1) shall be replaced by the following:

'1.   Pending the entry into force of the uniform electoral procedure or the procedure based on common principles referred to in Article 7 and subject to the other provisions of this Act, each Member State shall lay down appropriate procedures for filling any seat which falls vacant during the five-year term of office referred to in Article 3 for the remainder of that period.'

PART TWO

SIMPLIFICATION

Article 6

The Treaty establishing the European Community, including the annexes and protocols thereto, shall be amended in accordance with the provisions of this Article for the purpose of deleting lapsed provisions of the Treaty and adapting in consequence the text of certain of its provisions.

I. TEXT OF THE ARTICLES OF THE TREATY

1. In Article 3, point (a), the word 'elimination' shall be replaced by 'prohibition'.

2. Article 7 shall be repealed.

3. Article 7a shall be amended as follows:

    (a) the first and second paragraphs shall be numbered and thus become paragraphs 1 and 2;

    (b) in the new paragraph 1, the following references shall be deleted: '7b', '70(1)' and 'and 100b'; before the citation of Article 100a, the comma shall be replaced by the word 'and';

    (c) there shall be added a paragraph 3 with the wording of the second paragraph of Article 7b which reads as follows:

    '3.   The Council, acting by a qualified majority on a proposal from the Commission, shall determine the guidelines and conditions necessary to ensure balanced progress in all the sectors concerned.'.

4. Article 7b shall be repealed.

5. Article 8b shall be amended as follows:

    (a) in paragraph 1 the words 'to be adopted before 31 December 1994' shall be replaced by 'adopted';

    (b) in paragraph 2, first sentence, the reference to 'Article 138(3)' shall become 'Article 138(4)';

    (c) in paragraph 2, second sentence, the words 'to be adopted before 31 December 1993' shall be replaced by 'adopted'.

6. In Article 8c, second sentence, the words 'Before 31 December 1993, Member States ...' shall be replaced by 'Member States ...'.

7. In Article 8e, first paragraph, the words 'before 31 December 1993 and then,' shall be deleted, as well as the comma after the words 'every three years'.

8. In Article 9(2), the words 'The provisions of Chapter 1, Section 1, and of Chapter 2 ...' shall be replaced by 'The provisions of Article 12 and of Chapter 2 ...'.

9. In Article 10, paragraph 2 shall be deleted and paragraph 1 shall remain without a number.

10. Article 11 shall be repealed.

11. In Chapter 1, The Customs Union, the heading 'Section 1 — Elimination of customs duties between Member States' shall be deleted.

12. Article 12 shall be replaced by the following:

'*Article 12*

Customs duties on imports and exports and charges having equivalent effect shall be prohibited between Member States. This prohibition shall also apply to customs duties of a fiscal nature.'.

13. Articles 13 to 17 shall be repealed.

14. The heading 'Section 2 — Setting up of the Common Customs Tariff' shall be deleted.

15. Articles 18 to 27 shall be repealed.

16. Article 28 shall be replaced by the following:

'*Article 28*

Common Customs Tariff duties shall be fixed by the Council acting by a qualified majority on a proposal from the Commission.'.

17. In the introductory part of Article 29, the words 'this Section' shall be replaced by 'this Chapter'.

18. In the title of Chapter 2, the word 'Elimination' shall be replaced by 'Prohibition'.

19. In Article 30, the words 'shall, without prejudice to the following provisions, be prohibited ...' shall be replaced by 'shall be prohibited ...'.

20. Articles 31, 32 and 33 shall be repealed.

21. In Article 34, paragraph 2 shall be deleted and paragraph 1 shall remain without a number.

22. Article 35 shall be repealed.

23. In Article 36, the words 'The provisions of Articles 30 to 34' shall be replaced by 'The provisions of Articles 30 and 34'.

24. Article 37 shall be amended as follows:

   (a) in paragraph 1, first subparagraph, the word 'progressively' and the words 'when the transitional period has ended' shall be deleted;

   (b) in paragraph 2, the word 'abolition' shall be replaced by 'prohibition';

   (c) paragraphs 3, 5 and 6 shall be deleted and paragraph 4 shall become paragraph 3;

   (d) in the new paragraph 3, the words 'account being taken of the adjustments that will be possible and the specialization that will be needed with the passage of time.' shall be deleted and the comma after 'concerned' shall become a full stop.

25. Article 38 shall be amended as follows:

   (a) in paragraph 3, first sentence, the reference to Annex II shall be replaced by a reference to Annex I and the second sentence, beginning with the words 'Within two years of the entry into force ...' shall be deleted;

   (b) in paragraph 4, the words 'among the Member States.' shall be deleted.

26. Article 40 shall be amended as follows:

   (a) paragraph 1 shall be deleted and paragraphs 2, 3 and 4 shall become paragraphs 1, 2 and 3;

   (b) (does not concern the English language version);

   (c) in new paragraph 2, the reference to 'paragraph 2' shall become 'paragraph 1';

   (d) in new paragraph 3, the reference to 'paragraph 2' shall become 'paragraph 1';

27. Article 43 shall be amended as follows:

   (a) in paragraph 2, third subparagraph, the words 'acting unanimously during the first two stages and by a qualified majority thereafter' shall be replaced by 'acting by a qualified majority';

   (b) in paragraphs 2 and 3, the reference to 'Article 40(2)' shall become 'Article 40(1)'.

28. Articles 44 and 45 and Article 47 shall be repealed.

29. In Article 48(1), the words 'by the end of the transitional period at the latest' shall be deleted.

30. Article 49 shall be amended as follows:

   (a) in the introductory part, the words 'As soon as this Treaty enters into force, the Council ...' shall be replaced by 'The Council ...' and the words 'by progressive stages' together with the commas preceding and following those words shall be deleted;

   (b) in points (b) and (c) respectively, the words 'systematically and progressively' shall be deleted.

31. The first paragraph of Article 52 shall be amended as follows:

    (a) in the first sentence, the words 'abolished by progressive stages in the course of the transitional period' shall be replaced by the word 'prohibited';

    (b) in the second sentence, the words 'progressive abolition' shall be replaced by the word 'prohibition'.

32. Article 53 shall be repealed.

33. Article 54 shall be amended as follows:

    (a) paragraph 1 shall be deleted and paragraphs 2 and 3 shall become paragraphs 1 and 2;

    (b) in new paragraph 1, the words 'implement this general programme or, in the absence of such a programme, in order to achieve a stage in attaining' shall be replaced by 'attain'.

34. In Article 59, first paragraph, the words 'progressively abolished during the transitional period' shall be replaced by 'prohibited'.

35. In Article 61(2), the word 'progressive' shall be deleted.

36. Article 62 shall be repealed.

37. Article 63 shall be amended as follows:

    (a) paragraph 1 shall be deleted and paragraphs 2 and 3 shall become paragraphs 1 and 2;

    (b) in new paragraph 1, the words 'implement this general programme or, in the absence of such a programme, in order to achieve a stage in' shall be replaced by the word 'achieve' and the words 'unanimously until the end of the first stage and by a qualified majority thereafter' shall be replaced by the words 'by a qualified majority';

    (c) in new paragraph 2, the words 'As regards the proposals and decisions referred to in paragraphs 1 and 2' shall be replaced by 'As regards the directives referred to in paragraph 1'.

38. In Article 64, first paragraph, 'Article 63(2)' shall be replaced by 'Article 63(1)'.

39. Articles 67 to 73a, Article 73e and Article 73h shall be repealed.

40. Article 75(2) shall be deleted and paragraph 3 shall become paragraph 2.

41. In Article 76, the words 'when this Treaty enters into force' shall be replaced by 'on 1 January 1958 or, for acceding States, the date of their accession'.

42. Article 79 shall be amended as follows:

    (a) in paragraph 1 the words 'at the latest, before the end of the second stage' shall be deleted;

    (b) in paragraph 3, the words 'Within two years of the entry into force of this Treaty, the Council shall' shall be replaced by 'The Council shall'.

43. In Article 80(1), the words 'as from the beginning of the second stage' shall be deleted.

44. In Article 83, the words 'without prejudice to the powers of the transport section of the Economic and Social Committee.' shall be replaced by 'without prejudice to the powers of the Economic and Social Committee.'.

45. In Article 84(2), second subparagraph, the words 'procedural provisions of Article 75(1) and (3)' shall be replaced by 'procedural provisions of Article 75'.

46. In Article 87, the two subparagraphs of paragraph 1 shall be merged into a single paragraph. This new paragraph shall read as follows:

    '1.   The appropriate regulations or directives to give effect to the principles set out in Articles 85 and 86 shall be laid down by the Council, acting by a qualified majority on a proposal from the Commission and after consulting the European Parliament.'.

47. In Article 89(1), the words ', as soon as it takes up its duties,' shall be deleted.

48. After Article 90, the heading 'Section 2 — Dumping' shall be deleted.

49. Article 91 shall be repealed.

50. Before Article 92, the heading 'Section 3' shall be replaced by 'Section 2'.

51. In Article 92(3)(c), the second sentence, beginning 'However, the aids granted to ship-building . . .' and ending 'towards third countries;' shall be deleted and the remaining part of point (c) shall end with a semicolon.

52. In Article 95, the third paragraph shall be deleted.

53. Article 97 and Article 100b shall be repealed.

54. In Article 101, second paragraph, the words 'acting unanimously during the first stage and by a qualified majority thereafter' shall be replaced by 'acting by a qualified majority'.

55. In Article 109e(2)(a), first indent, the following words shall be deleted: ', without prejudice to Article 73e,'.

56. Article 109f shall be amended as follows:

   (a) in paragraph 1, second subparagraph, the words 'on a recommendation from, as the case may be, the Committee of Governors of the central banks of the Member States (hereinafter referred to as "Committee of Governors") or the Council of the EMI' shall be replaced by 'on a recommendation from the Council of the EMI';

   (b) in paragraph 1, the fourth subparagraph which states 'The Committee of Governors shall be dissolved at the start of the second stage.' shall be deleted;

   (c) in paragraph 8, the second subparagraph which states 'Where this Treaty provides for a consultative role for the EMI, references to the EMI shall be read, before 1 January 1994, as referring to the Committee of Governors.' shall be deleted.

57. Article 112 shall be amended as follows:

   (a) in paragraph 1, first subparagraph, the words 'before the end of the transitional period' shall be deleted;

   (b) in paragraph 1, second subparagraph, the words 'acting unanimously until the end of the second stage and by a qualified majority thereafter' shall be replaced by 'acting by a qualified majority'.

58. In Article 129c(1), first subparagraph, third indent, the words 'Cohesion Fund to be set up no later than 31 December 1993' shall be replaced by 'Cohesion Fund set up'.

59. In Article 130d, second paragraph, the words 'The Council, acting in accordance with the same procedure, shall before 31 December 1993 set up a Cohesion Fund to' shall be replaced by 'A Cohesion Fund set up by the Council in accordance with the same procedure shall'.

60. In Article 130s, paragraph 5, second indent, the words 'Cohesion Fund to be set up no later than 31 December 1993 pursuant to Article 130d' shall be replaced by 'Cohesion Fund set up pursuant to Article 130d.'.

61. In Article 130w, paragraph 3, the words 'ACP-EEC Convention' shall be replaced by 'ACP-EC Convention'.

62. In Article 131, first paragraph, the words 'Belgium' and 'Italy' shall be deleted and the reference to Annex IV shall be replaced by a reference to Annex II.

63. Article 133 shall be amended as follows:

   (a) in paragraph 1, the words 'completely abolished' shall be replaced by the word 'prohibited' and the words 'progressive abolition' shall be replaced by the word 'prohibition';

(b) in paragraph 2, the words 'progressively abolished' shall be replaced by the word 'prohibited' and the references to Articles 13, 14, 15 and 17 shall be deleted with the result that the paragraph ends with the words '. . . in accordance with the provisions of Article 12.';

(c) in paragraph 3, second subparagraph, the words 'shall nevertheless be progressively reduced to' shall be replaced by 'may not exceed' and the second sentence beginning 'The percentages and the timetable . . .' and ending with 'importing country or territory.' shall be deleted;

(d) in paragraph 4, the words 'when this Treaty enters into force' shall be deleted.

64. Article 136 shall be replaced by the following:

'Article 136

The Council, acting unanimously, shall, on the basis of the experience acquired under the association of the countries and territories with the Community and of the principles set out in this Treaty, lay down provisions as regards the detailed rules and the procedure for the association of the countries and territories with the Community.'.

65. Article 138 shall be amended as follows, to include Article 1, Article 2 as amended by Article 5 of this Treaty, and Article 3(1) of the Act concerning the election of the representatives of the European Parliament by direct universal suffrage, annexed to the Council Decision of 20 September 1976; Annex II of that Act shall continue to be applied:

(a) in the place of paragraphs 1 and 2, which lapsed in accordance with Article 14 of the Act concerning the election of the representatives of the European Parliament, there shall be inserted the text of Articles 1 and 2 of the said Act as paragraphs 1 and 2; the new paragraphs 1 and 2 shall read as follows:

'1.   The representatives in the European Parliament of the peoples of the States brought together in the Community shall be elected by direct universal suffrage.

2.   The number of representatives elected in each Member State shall be as follows:

Belgium	25
Denmark	16
Germany	99
Greece	25
Spain	64
France	87
Ireland	15
Italy	87
Luxembourg	6
Netherlands	31
Austria	21
Portugal	25
Finland	16
Sweden	22
United Kingdom	87.

In the event of amendments to this paragraph, the number of representatives elected in each Member State must ensure appropriate representation of the peoples of the States brought together in the Community.';

(b) after the new paragraphs 1 and 2, there shall be inserted the text of Article 3(1) of the aforesaid Act as paragraph 3; the new paragraph 3 shall read as follows:

'3.   Representatives shall be elected for a term of five years.';

(c) the existing paragraph 3 as amended by Article 2 of this Treaty shall become paragraph 4;

(d) paragraph 4 as added by Article 2 of this Treaty shall become paragraph 5.

66. Article 158(3) shall be deleted.

67. In Article 166, first paragraph, the words 'as from the date of accession' shall be replaced by 'as from 1 January 1995'.

68. In Article 188b(3), the second subparagraph, commencing 'However, when the first appointments . . .' shall be deleted.

69. In Article 197, the second paragraph, commencing 'In particular, it shall . . .' shall be deleted.

70. In Article 207, the second, third, fourth and fifth paragraphs shall be deleted.

71. In the place of Article 212 there shall be inserted the text of Article 24(1), second subparagraph, of the Treaty establishing a Single Council and a Single Commission of the European Communities; the new Article 212 shall accordingly read as follows:

'*Article 212*

The Council shall, acting by a qualified majority on a proposal from the Commission and after consulting the other institutions concerned, lay down the Staff Regulations of officials of the European Communities and the Conditions of Employment of other servants of those Communities.'.

72. In the place of Article 218 there shall be inserted the adapted text of Article 28, first paragraph, of the Treaty establishing a Single Council and a Single Commission of the European Communities; the new Article 218 shall accordingly read as follows:

'*Article 218*

The Community shall enjoy in the territories of the Member States such privileges and immunities as are necessary for the performance of its tasks, under the conditions laid down in the Protocol of 8 April 1965 on the privileges and immunities of the European Communities. The same shall apply to the European Central Bank, the European Monetary Institute, and the European Investment Bank.'.

73. In Article 221 the words 'Within three years of the entry into force of this Treaty, Member States shall accord . . .' shall be replaced by 'Member States shall accord . . .'.

74. In Article 223, paragraphs 2 and 3 shall be merged and replaced by the following:

'2.   The Council may, acting unanimously on a proposal from the Commission, make changes to the list, which it drew up on 15 April 1958, of the products to which the provisions of paragraph 1(b) apply.'.

75. Article 226 shall be repealed.

76. Article 227 shall be amended as follows:

(a) in paragraph 3, the reference to Annex IV shall be replaced by a reference to Annex II;

(b) after paragraph 4, a new paragraph shall be inserted as follows:

'5.   The provisions of this Treaty shall apply to the Åland Islands in accordance with the provisions set out in Protocol No 2 to the Act concerning the conditions of accession of the Republic of Austria, the Republic of Finland and the Kingdom of Sweden.';

(c) the former paragraph 5 shall become paragraph 6 and point (d) thereof, concerning the Åland Islands shall be deleted; point (c) shall end with a full stop.

77. In Article 229, first paragraph, the words 'organs of the United Nations, of its specialised agencies and of the General Agreement on Tariffs and Trade.' shall be replaced by 'organs of the United Nations and of its specialised agencies.'

78. In Article 234, first paragraph, the words 'before the entry into force of this Treaty' shall be replaced by 'before 1 January 1958 or, for acceding States, before the date of their accession'.

79. The heading preceding Article 241 entitled 'Setting up of the institutions' shall be deleted.

80. Articles 241 to 246 shall be repealed.

81. In Article 248 a new paragraph shall be added as follows:

'Pursuant to the Accession Treaties, the Danish, English, Finnish, Greek, Irish, Portuguese, Spanish and Swedish versions of this Treaty shall also be authentic.'.

II. ANNEXES

1. Annex I 'Lists A to G referred to in Articles 19 and 20 of the Treaty' shall be deleted.

2. Annex II 'List referred to in Article 38 of the Treaty' shall become Annex I and the reference to 'Annes II to the Treaty' under numbers ex 22.08 and ex 22.09 shall become a reference to 'Annex I to the Treaty'.

3. Annex III 'List of invisible transactions referred to in Article 73h of the Treaty' shall be deleted.

4. Annex IV 'Overseas countries and territories to which the provisions of Part IV of the Treaty apply' shall become Annex II. It is brought up to date and reads as follows:

'*ANNEX II*

OVERSEAS COUNTRIES AND TERRITORIES

to which the provisions of Part IV of the Treaty apply

— Greenland,

— New Caledonia and Dependencies,

— French Polynesia,

— French Southern and Antarctic Territories,

— Wallis and Futuna Islands,

— Mayotte,

— Saint Pierre and Miquelon,

— Aruba,

— Netherlands Antilles:

— Bonaire,

— Curaçao,

— Saba,

— Sint Eustatius,

— Sint Maarten,

— Anguilla,

— Cayman Islands,

— Falkland Islands,

— South Georgia and the South Sandwich Islands,

— Montserrat,

— Pitcairn,

— Saint Helena and Dependencies,

— British Antarctic Territory,

— British Indian Ocean Territory,

— Turks and Caicos Islands,

— British Virgin Islands,

— Bermuda.'.

III. PROTOCOLS AND OTHER ACTS

1. The following protocols and acts shall be repealed:

(a) Protocol amending the Protocol on the privileges and immunities of the European Communities;

(b) Protocol on German internal trade and connected problems;

(c) Protocol on certain provisions relating to France;

(d) Protocol on the Grand Duchy of Luxembourg;

(e) Protocol on the treatment to be applied to products within the province of the European Coal and Steel Community in respect of Algeria and the overseas departments of the French Republic;

(f) Protocol on mineral oils and certain of their derivatives;

(g) Protocol on the application of the Treaty establishing the European Community to the non-European parts of the Kingdom of the Netherlands;

(h) Implementing Convention on the Association of the Overseas Countries and Territories with the Community;

    — Protocol on the tariff quota for imports of bananas (ex 08.01 of the Brussels Nomenclature);

    — Protocol on the tariff quota for imports of raw coffee (ex 09.01 of the Brussels Nomenclature).

2. At the end of the Protocol on the Statute of the European Investment Bank, the list of signatories shall be deleted.

3. Protocol on the Statute of the Court of Justice of the European Community shall be amended as follows:

(a) the words 'HAVE DESIGNATED as their plenipotentiaries for this purpose:' and the list of Heads of State and their plenipotentiaries shall be deleted;

(b) the words 'WHO, having exchanged their full powers, found in good and due form,' shall be deleted;

(c) in Article 3, the adapted text of Article 21 of the Protocol on the privileges and immunities of the European Communities shall be added as a fourth paragraph; this new fourth paragraph shall accordingly read as follows:

'Articles 12 to 15 and 18 of the Protocol on the privileges and immunities of the European Communities shall apply to the Judges, Advocates-General, Registrar and Assistant Rapporteurs of the Court of Justice, without prejudice to the provisions relating to immunity from legal proceedings of Judges which are set out in the preceding paragraphs.';

(d) Article 57 shall be repealed;

(e) the concluding formula 'IN WITNESS WHEREOF, the undersigned Plenipotentiaries have signed this Protocol.' shall be deleted;

(f) the list of signatories shall be deleted.

4. In Article 40 of the Protocol on the Statute of the European System of Central Banks and of the European Central Bank, the words 'annexed to the Treaty establishing a Single Council and a Single Commission of the European Communities' shall be deleted.

5. In Article 21 of the Protocol on the Statute of the European Monetary Institute, the words 'annexed to the Treaty establishing a Single Council and a Single Commission of the European Communities' shall be deleted.

6. The Protocol on Italy shall be amended as follows:

(a) in the last paragraph commencing 'RECOGNISE that in the event . . .', the reference to Articles 108 and 109 shall be replaced by a reference to Articles 109h and 109i;

(b) the list of signatories shall be deleted.

7. The Protocol on goods originating in and coming from certain countries and enjoying special treatment when imported into a Member State shall be amended as follows:

(a) in the introductory part of point 1:

— the words 'applicable, at the time of the entry into force of this Treaty' shall be replaced by 'applicable on 1 January 1958.';

— after the words 'to imports', the text of point (a) shall follow on immediately; the text resulting therefrom shall read as follows:

'... to imports into the Benelux countries of goods originating in and coming from Suriname or the Netherlands Antilles;';

(b) in point 1, points (a), (b) and (c) shall be deleted;

(c) in point 3, the words 'Before the end of the first year after the entry into force of this Treaty, Member States ...' shall be replaced by 'Member States';

(d) the list of signatories shall be deleted.

8. The Protocol concerning imports into the European Community of petroleum products refined in the Netherlands Antilles shall be amended as follows:

(a) the concluding formula 'IN WITNESS WHEREOF the undersigned Plenipotentiaries have placed their signatures below this Protocol.' shall be deleted;

(b) the list of signatories shall be deleted.

9. In the Protocol on special arrangements for Greenland, Article 3 shall be repealed.

Article 7

The Treaty establishing the European Coal and Steel Community, including the annexes, protocols and other acts annexed thereto, shall be amended in accordance with the provisions of this Article for the purpose of deleting lapsed provisions of the Treaty and adapting in consequence the text of certain of its provisions.

I. TEXT OF THE ARTICLES OF THE TREATY

1. In Article 2, second paragraph, the word 'progressively' shall be deleted.

2. In Article 4, in the introductory part, the words 'abolished and' shall be deleted.

3. Article 7 shall be amended as follows:

(a) in the first indent, the words 'a HIGH AUTHORITY (hereinafter referred to as "the Commission")' shall be replaced by 'a COMMISSION';

(b) in the second indent, the words 'a COMMON ASSEMBLY (hereinafter referred to as "the European Parliament")' shall be replaced by 'a EUROPEAN PARLIAMENT';

(c) in the third indent, the words 'a SPECIAL COUNCIL OF MINISTERS (hereinafter referred to as "the Council")' shall be replaced by 'a COUNCIL';

4. Article 10(3) shall be deleted.

5. In Article 16, the first and second paragraphs shall be deleted.

6. Article 21 shall be amended as follows, to include Article 1, Article 2 as amended by Article 5 of this Treaty, and Article 3(1) of the Act concerning the election of the representatives of the European Parliament by direct universal suffrage, annexed to the Council Decision of 20 September 1976; Annex II of that Act shall continue to be applied:

(a) in the place of paragraphs 1 and 2, which lapsed in accordance with Article 14 of the Act concerning the election of the representatives of the European Parliament, there shall be inserted the text of Articles 1 and 2 of the said Act as paragraphs 1 and 2; the new paragraphs 1 and 2 shall read as follows:

'1.   The representatives in the European Parliament of the peoples of the States brought together in the Community shall be elected by direct universal suffrage.

2.   The number of representatives elected in each Member State shall be as follows:

Belgium	25
Denmark	16
Germany	99
Greece	25
Spain	64
France	87
Ireland	15
Italy	87
Luxembourg	6
Netherlands	31
Austria	21
Portugal	25
Finland	16
Sweden	22
United Kingdom	87.

In the event of amendments to this paragraph, the number of representatives elected in each Member State must ensure appropriate representation of the peoples of the States brought together in the Community.';

(b) after the new paragraphs 1 and 2, there shall be inserted the text of Article 3(1) of the aforesaid Act as paragraph 3; the new paragraph 3 shall read as follows:

'3.   Representatives shall be elected for a term of five years.';

(c) the existing paragraph 3 as amended by Article 3 of this Treaty shall become paragraph 4;

(d) paragraph 4 as added by Article 3 of this Treaty shall become paragraph 5.

7. In Article 32a, first paragraph, the words 'the date of accession' shall be replaced by '1 January 1995'.

8. In Article 45b(3), the second subparagraph commencing 'However, when the first appointments . . .' shall be deleted.

9. In Article 50, the adapted text of paragraphs 2 and 3 of Article 20 of the Treaty establishing a Single Council and a Single Commission of the European Communities shall be inserted as new paragraphs 4 and 5; the new paragraphs 4 and 5 shall accordingly read as follows:

'4.   The portion of the expenditure of the budget of the Communities covered by the levies provided for in Article 49 shall be fixed at 18 million units of account.

The Commission shall submit annually to the Council a report on the basis of which the Council shall examine whether there is reason to adjust this figure to changes in the budget of the Communities. The Council shall act by the majority laid down in the first sentence of the fourth paragraph of Article 28. The adjustment shall be made on the basis of an assessment of developments in expenditure arising from the application of this Treaty.

5.   The portion of the levies assigned to cover expenditure under the budget of the Communities shall be allocated by the Commission for the implementation of that budget in accordance with the timetable provided for in the financial regulations adopted pursuant to Article 209(b) of the Treaty establishing the European Community and Article 183(b) of the Treaty establishing the Atomic Energy Community.'.

10. Article 52 shall be repealed.

11. In the place of Article 76 there shall be inserted the adapted text of Article 28, first paragraph, of the Treaty establishing a Single Council and a Single Commission of the European Communities; the new Article 76 shall accordingly read as follows:

'*Article 76*

The Community shall enjoy in the territories of the Member States such privileges and immunities as are necessary for the performance of its tasks, under the conditions laid down in the Protocol of 8 April 1965 on the privileges and immunities of the European Communities.'.

12. Article 79 shall be amended as follows:

(a) in the second sentence of the first paragraph, the part of the sentence which commences 'as regards the Saar . . .' shall be deleted and the semicolon shall be replaced by a full stop;

(b) after the first paragraph, a second paragraph shall be inserted as follows:

'The provisions of this Treaty shall apply to the Åland Islands in accordance with the provisions of Protocol No 2 of the Act concerning the conditions of accession of the Republic of Austria, the Republic of Finland and the Kingdom of Sweden.';

(c) in the existing second paragraph, in the introductory part, the words 'Notwithstanding the preceding paragraph:' shall be replaced by 'Notwithstanding the preceding paragraphs:';

(d) in the existing second paragraph, point (d) concerning the Åland Islands shall be deleted.

13. In Article 84, the words 'Treaty and its Annexes, of the Protocols annexed thereto and of the Convention on the transitional Provisions.' shall be replaced by 'Treaty and its Annexes and of the Protocols annexed thereto.'

14. Article 85 shall be repealed.

15. In Article 93, the words 'Organisation for European Economic Cooperation' shall be replaced by 'Organisation for Economic Cooperation and Development'.

16. In Article 95, third paragraph, the words 'If, after the end of the transitional period provided in the Convention on the Transitional Provisions, unforeseen difficulties ...' shall be replaced by 'If unforeseen difficulties ...'.

17. In Article 97, the wording 'This Treaty is concluded for a period of 50 years from its entry into force.' shall be replaced by 'This Treaty shall expire on 23 July 2002.'.

II. TEXT OF ANNEX III 'Special steels'

At the end of Annex III, the initials of the plenipotentiaries of the Heads of State and Government shall be deleted.

III. PROTOCOLS AND OTHER ACTS ANNEXED TO THE TREATY

1. The following acts shall be repealed:

(a) Exchange of letters between the Government of the Federal Republic of Germany and the Government of the French Republic concerning the Saar;

(b) Convention on the Transitional Provisions.

2. The Protocol on the Statute of the Court of Justice of the European Coal and Steel Community shall be amended as follows:

(a) Titles I and II of the Protocol shall be replaced by the text of Titles I and II of the Protocol on the Statute of the Court of Justice of the European Community annexed to the Treaty establishing the European Community;

(b) Article 56 shall be repealed and the heading 'Transitional provision' which precedes it shall be deleted;

(c) the list of signatories shall be deleted.

3. The Protocol on relations with the Council of Europe shall be amended as follows:

(a) Article 1 shall be repealed;

(b) the list of signatories shall be deleted.

Article 8

The Treaty establishing the European Atomic Energy Community, including the annexes and protocols thereto, shall be amended in accordance with the provisions of this Article for the purpose of deleting lapsed provisions of the Treaty and adapting in consequence the text of certain of its provisions.

I. TEXT OF THE ARTICLES OF THE TREATY

1. In Article 76, second paragraph, the words 'after the entry into force of this Treaty' shall be replaced by 'after 1 January 1958'.

2. In the introductory part to the first paragraph of Article 93, the words 'Member States shall abolish between themselves, one year after the entry into force of this Treaty, all customs duties ...' shall be replaced by 'Member States shall prohibit between themselves all customs duties ...'.

3. Articles 94 and 95 shall be repealed.

4. In Article 98, second paragraph, the words 'Within two years of the entry into force of this Treaty, the Council ...' shall be replaced by 'The Council ...'.

5. Article 100 shall be repealed.

6. Article 104 shall be amended as follows:

(a) in the first paragraph, the words 'after the entry into force of this Treaty' shall be replaced by 'after 1 January 1958 or, for acceding States, after the date of their accession,';

(b) in the second paragraph the words 'after the entry into force of this Treaty, within the purview thereof' shall be replaced by 'after the dates referred to in the first paragraph, within the scope of this Treaty'.

7. Article 105 shall be amended as follows:

   (a) in the first paragraph, the words 'concluded before its entry into force by a Member State' shall be replaced by 'concluded before 1 January 1958 or, for acceding States, before the date of their accession, by a Member State'. At the end of that paragraph the words 'the entry into force of this Treaty' shall be replaced by 'the aforesaid dates';

   (b) in the second paragraph, the words 'concluded between the signature and the entry into force of this Treaty' shall be replaced by 'concluded between 25 March 1957 and 1 January 1958 or, for acceding States, between the signature of the instrument of accession and the date of their accession'.

8. In Article 106, first paragraph, the words 'before the entry into force of this Treaty' shall be replaced by 'before 1 January 1958 or, for acceding States, before the date of their accession'.

9. Article 108 shall be amended as follows, to include Article 1, Article 2 as amended by Article 5 of this Treaty, and Article 3(1) of the Act concerning the election of the representatives of the European Parliament by direct universal suffrage, annexed to the Council Decision of 20 September 1976; Annex II of that Act shall continue to be applied:

   (a) in the place of paragraphs 1 and 2, which lapsed in accordance with Article 14 of the Act concerning the election of the representatives of the European Parliament, there shall be inserted the text of Articles 1 and 2 of the said Act as paragraphs 1 and 2; the new paragraphs 1 and 2 shall read as follows:

   '1.   The representatives in the European Parliament of the peoples of the States brought together in the Community shall be elected by direct universal suffrage.

   2.   The number of representatives elected in each Member State shall be as follows:

Belgium	25
Denmark	16
Germany	99
Greece	25
Spain	64
France	87
Ireland	15
Italy	87
Luxembourg	6
Netherlands	31
Austria	21
Portugal	25
Finland	16
Sweden	22
United Kingdom	87.

In the event of amendments to this paragraph, the number of representatives elected in each Member State must ensure appropriate representation of the peoples of the States brought together in the Community.';

(b) after the new paragraphs 1 and 2, there shall be inserted the text of Article 3(1) of the aforesaid Act as paragraph 3; the new paragraph 3 shall read as follows:

'3.   Representatives shall be elected for a term of five years.';

(c) the existing paragraph 3 as amended by Article 4 of this Treaty shall become paragraph 4;

(d) paragraph 4 as added by Article 4 of this Treaty shall become paragraph 5.

10. In Article 127, paragraph 3 shall be deleted.

11. In Article 138, first paragraph, the words 'the date of accession' shall be replaced by '1 January 1995'.

12. In Article 160b(3), the second subparagraph commencing 'However, when the first appointments . . .' shall be deleted.

13. In Article 181, the second, third and fourth paragraphs shall be deleted.

14. In the place of Article 191 there shall be inserted the adapted text of Article 28, first paragraph, of the Treaty establishing a Single Council and a Single Commission of the European Communities; the new Article 191 shall accordingly read as follows:

'*Article 191*

The Community shall enjoy in the territories of the Member States such privileges and immunities as are necessary for the performance of its tasks, under the conditions laid down in the Protocol of 8 April 1965 on the privileges and immunities of the European Communities.'.

15. Article 198 shall be amended as follows:

(a) after the second paragraph there shall be inserted a third paragraph as follows:

'The provisions of this Treaty shall apply to the Åland Islands in accordance with the provisions set out in Protocol No 2 to the Act concerning the conditions of accession of the Republic of Austria, the Republic of Finland and the Kingdom of Sweden.';

(b) in the existing third paragraph, point (e) concerning the Åland Islands shall be deleted.

16. In Article 199, first paragraph, the words 'and of the General Agreement on Tariffs and Trade' shall be replaced by 'and of the World Trade Organisation'.

17. Title VI, 'Provisions relating to the initial period', comprising Section 1, 'Setting up of the institutions', Section 2, 'Provisions for the initial application of this Treaty' and Section 3, 'Transitional provisions' and Articles 209 to 223, shall be repealed.

18. In Article 225 there shall be added a new paragraph as follows:

'Pursuant to the Accession treaties the Danish, English, Finnish, Greek, Irish, Portuguese, Spanish and Swedish versions of this Treaty shall also be authentic.'.

II. ANNEXES

Annex V, 'Initial research and training programme referred to in Article 215 of this Treaty' including the table 'Breakdown by main headings . . .' shall be deleted.

III. PROTOCOLS

1. The Protocol on the application of the Treaty establishing the European Atomic Energy Community to the non-European parts of the Kingdom of the Netherlands shall be repealed.

2. The Protocol on the Statute of the Court of Justice of the European Atomic Energy Community shall be amended as follows:

(a) the words 'HAVE DESIGNATED as their Plenipotentiaries for this Purpose:' and the list of Heads of State and their plenipotentiaries shall be deleted;

(b) the words 'WHO, having exchanged their full powers, found in good and due form,' shall be deleted;

(c) in Article 3, the adapted text of Article 21 of the Protocol on the privileges and immunities of the European Communities shall be added as a fourth paragraph; this new fourth paragraph shall accordingly read as follows:

'Articles 12 to 15 and 18 of the Protocol on the privileges and immunities of the European Community shall apply to the Judges, Advocates-General, Registrar and Assistant Rapporteurs of the Court of Justice, without prejudice to the provisions relating to immunity from legal proceedings of Judges which are set out in the preceding paragraphs.';

(d) Article 58 shall be repealed;

(e) the concluding formula 'IN WITNESS WHEREOF, the undersigned Plenipotentiaries have signed this Protocol.' shall be deleted;

(f) the list of signatories shall be deleted.

Article 9

1.   Without prejudice to the paragraphs following hereinafter, which have as their purpose to retain the essential elements of their provisions, the Convention of 25 March 1957 on

certain institutions common to the European Communities and the Treaty of 8 April 1965 establishing a Single Council and a Single Commission of the European Communities, but with the exception of the Protocol referred to in paragraph 5, shall be repealed.

2.   The powers conferred on the European Parliament, the Council, the Commission, the Court of Justice and the Court of Auditors by the Treaty establishing the European Community, the Treaty establishing the European Coal and Steel Community and the Treaty establishing the European Atomic Energy Community shall be exercised by the single institutions under the conditions laid down respectively by the said Treaties and this Article.

The functions conferred on the Economic and Social Committee by the Treaty establishing the European Community and the Treaty establishing the European Atomic Energy Community shall be exercised by a single committee under the conditions laid down respectively by the said Treaties. The provisions of Articles 193 and 197 of the Treaty establishing the European Community shall apply to that Committee.

3.   The officials and other staff of the European Communities shall form part of the single administration of those Communities and shall be governed by the provisions adopted pursuant to Article 212 of the Treaty establishing the European Community.

4.   The European Communities shall enjoy in the territories of the Member States such privileges and immunities as are necessary for the performance of their tasks under the conditions set out in the Protocol referred to in paragraph 5. The position shall be the same as regards the European Central Bank, the European Monetary Institute and the European Investment Bank.

5.   In the Protocol of 8 April 1965 on the privileges and immunities of the European Communities there shall be inserted an Article 23, as laid down in Protocol amending the said Protocol; that Article reads as follows:

'*Article 23*

This Protocol shall also apply to the European Central Bank, to the members of its organs and to its staff, without prejudice to the provisions of the Protocol on the Statute of the European System of Central Banks and the European Central Bank.

The European Central Bank shall, in addition, be exempt from any form of taxation or imposition of a like nature on the occasion of any increase in its capital and from the various formalities which may be connected therewith in the State where the Bank has its seat. The activities of the Bank and of its organs carried on in accordance with the Statute of the European System of Central Banks and of the European Central Bank shall not be subject to any turnover tax.

The above provisions shall also apply to the European Monetary Institute. Its dissolution or liquidation shall not give rise to any imposition.'.

6.   The revenue and expenditure of the European Community, the administrative expenditure of the European Coal and Steel Community and the revenue relating thereto and the revenue and expenditure of the European Atomic Energy Community, except for those of the Supply Agency and Joint Undertakings, shall be shown in the budget of the European Communities, under the conditions laid down respectively in the Treaties establishing the three Communities.

7.   Without prejudice to the application of Article 216 of the Treaty establishing the European Community, Article 77 of the Treaty establishing the European Coal and Steel Community, Article 189 of the Treaty establishing the European Atomic Energy Community and the second paragraph of Article 1 of the Protocol on the Statute of the European Investment Bank, the representatives of the Governments of the Member States shall adopt by common accord the necessary provisions for the purpose of dealing with certain problems particular to the Grand Duchy of Luxembourg which arise from the creation of a Single Council and a Single Commission of the European Communities.

Article 10

1.   The repeal or deletion in this Part of lapsed provisions of the Treaty establishing the European Community, the Treaty establishing the European Coal and Steel Community and the Treaty establishing the European Atomic Energy Community as in force before the entry into force of this Treaty of Amsterdam and the adaptation of certain of their provisions shall not bring about any change in the legal effects of the provisions of those Treaties, in particular the legal effects arising from the time limits laid down by the said Treaties, nor of Accession Treaties.

2.   There shall be no change in the legal effects of the acts in force adopted on the basis of the said Treaties.

3.   The position shall be the same as regards the repeal of the Convention of 25 March 1957 on certain institutions common to the European Communities and the repeal of the Treaty of 8 April 1965 establishing a Single Council and a Single Commission of the European Communities.

Article 11

The provisions of the Treaty establishing the European Community, the Treaty establishing the European Coal and Steel Community and the Treaty establishing the European Atomic Energy Community relating to the powers of the Court of Justice of the European Communities and to the exercise of those powers shall apply to the provisions of this Part and to the Protocol on privileges and immunities referred to in Article 9(5).

PART THREE

GENERAL AND FINAL PROVISIONS

Article 12

1.   The articles, titles and sections of the Treaty on European Union and of the Treaty establishing the European Community, as amended by the provisions of this Treaty, shall be renumbered in accordance with the tables of equivalences set out in the Annex to this Treaty, which shall form an integral part thereof.

2.   The cross references to articles, titles and sections in the Treaty on European Union and in the Treaty establishing the European Community, as well as between them, shall be adapted in consequence. The same shall apply as regards references to articles, titles and sections of those treaties contained in the other Community treaties.

3.   The references to the articles, titles and sections of the Treaties referred to in paragraph 2 contained in other instruments or acts shall be understood as references to the articles, titles and sections of the Treaties as renumbered pursuant to paragraph 1 and, respectively, to the paragraphs of the said articles, as renumbered by certain provisions of Article 6.

4.   References, contained in other instruments or acts, to paragraphs of articles of the Treaties referred to in Articles 7 and 8 shall be understood as referring to those paragraphs as renumbered by certain provisions of the said Articles 7 and 8.

Article 13

This Treaty is concluded for an unlimited period.

Article 14

1.   This Treaty shall be ratified by the High Contracting Parties in accordance with their respective constitutional requirements. The instruments of ratification shall be deposited with the Government of the Italian Republic.

2.   This Treaty shall enter into force on the first day of the second month following that in which the instrument of ratification is deposited by the last signatory State to fulfil that formality.

Article 15

This Treaty, drawn up in a single original in the Danish, Dutch, English, Finnish, French, German, Greek, Irish, Italian, Portuguese, Spanish and Swedish languages, the texts in each of these languages being equally authentic, shall be deposited in the archives of the Government of the Italian Republic, which will transmit a certified copy to each of the governments of the other signatory States.

En fe de lo cual, los plenipotenciarios abajo firmantes suscriben el presente Tratado.

Til bekræftelse heraf har undertegnede befuldmægtigede underskrevet denne traktat.

Zu Urkund dessen haben die unterzeichneten Bevollmächtigten ihre Unterschriften unter diesen Vertrag gesetzt.

Εις πίστωση των ανωτέρω, οι υπογεγραμμένοι πληρεξούσιοι υπέγραψαν την παρούσα Συνθήκη.

In witness whereof the undersigned Plenipotentiaries have signed this Treaty.

En foi de quoi, les plénipotentiaires soussignés ont apposé leurs signatures au bas du présent traité.

Dá fhianú sin, chuir na Lánchumhachtaigh thíos-sínithe a lámh leis an gConradh seo.

In fede di che, i plenipotenziari sottoscritti hanno apposto le loro firme in calce al presente trattato.

Ten blijke waarvan de ondergetekende gevolmachtigden hun handtekening onder dit Verdrag hebben gesteld.

Em fé do que, os plenipotenciários abaixo assinados apuseram as suas assinaturas no presente Tratado.

Tämän vakuudeksi alla mainitut täysivaltaiset edustajat ovat allekirjoittaneet tämän sopimuksen.

Til bevis härpå har undertecknade befullmäktigade undertecknat detta fördrag.

Hecho en Amsterdam, el dos de octubre de mil novecientos noventa y siete.

Udfærdiget i Amsterdam, den anden oktober nittenhundrede og syvoghalvfems.

Geschehen zu Amsterdam am zweiten Oktober neunzehnhundertsiebenundneunzig.

Έγινε στο Άμστερνταμ, στις δύο Οκτωβρίου του έτους χίλια εννιακόσια ενενήντα επτά.

Done at Amsterdam this second day of October in the year one thousand nine hundred and ninety-seven.

Fait à Amsterdam, le deux octobre de l'an mil neuf cent quatre-vingt-dix-sept.

Arna dhéanamh in Amstardam ar an dara lá de Dheireadh Fómhair sa bhliain míle naoi gcéad nócha a seacht.

Fatto ad Amsterdam, addì due ottobre millenovecentonovantasette.

Gedaan te Amsterdam, de tweede oktober negentienhonderd zevenennegentig.

Feito em Amesterdão, em dois de Outubro de mil novecentos e noventa e sete.

Tehty Amsterdamissa 2 päivänä lokakuuta vuonna tuhatyhdeksänsataayhdeksänkymmentäseitsemän.

Utfärdat i Amsterdam den andra oktober år nittonhundranittiosju.

Pour Sa Majesté le Roi des Belges
Voor Zijne Majesteit de Koning der Belgen
Für Seine Majestät den König der Belgier

Cette signature engage également la Communauté française, la Communauté flamande, la Communauté germanophone, la Région wallonne, la Région flamande et la Région de Bruxelles-Capitale.

Deze handtekening verbindt eveneens de Vlaamse Gemeenschap, de Franse Gemeenschap, de Duitstalige Gemeenschap, het Vlaamse Gewest, het Waalse Gewest en het Brusselse Hoofdstedelijke Gewest.

Diese Unterschrift bindet zugleich die Deutschsprachige Gemeinschaft, die Flämische Gemeinschaft, die Französische Gemeinschaft, die Wallonische Region, die Flämische Region und die Region Brüssel-Hauptstadt.

For Hendes Majestæt Danmarks Dronning

Für den Präsidenten der Bundesrepublik Deutschland

Για τον Πρόεδρο της Ελληνικής Δημοκρατίας

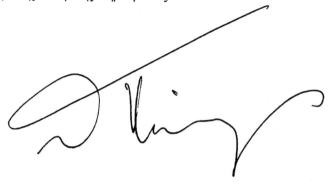

Por Su Majestad el Rey de España

Pour le Président de la République française

Thar ceann an Choimisiúin arna údarú le hAirteagal 14 de Bhunreacht na hÉireann chun cumhachtaí agus feidhmeanna Uachtarán na hÉireann a oibriú agus a chomhlíonadh
For the Commission authorised by Article 14 of the Constitution of Ireland to exercise and perform the powers and functions of the President of Ireland

Per il Presidente della Repubblica italiana

Pour Son Altesse Royale le Grand-Duc de Luxembourg

Voor Hare Majesteit de Koningin der Nederlanden

Für den Bundespräsidenten der Republik Österreich

Pelo Presidente da República Portuguesa

Suomen Tasavallan Presidentin puolesta
För Republiken Finlands President

För Hans Majestät Konungen av Sverige

For Her Majesty the Queen of the United Kingdom of Great Britain and Northern Ireland

—

ANNEX

TABLES OF EQUIVALENCES REFERRED TO IN ARTICLE 12 OF THE TREATY OF AMSTERDAM

A. Treaty on European Union

Previous numbering	New numbering	Previous numbering	New numbering
TITLE I	**TITLE I**	**TITLE VI (***)**	**TITLE VI**
Article A	Article 1	Article K.1	Article 29
Article B	Article 2	Article K.2	Article 30
Article C	Article 3	Article K.3	Article 31
Article D	Article 4	Article K.4	Article 32
Article E	Article 5	Article K.5	Article 33
Article F	Article 6	Article K.6	Article 34
Article F.1 (*)	Article 7	Article K.7	Article 35
TITLE II	**TITLE II**	Article K.8	Article 36
Article G	Article 8	Article K.9	Article 37
TITLE III	**TITLE III**	Article K.10	Article 38
Article H	Article 9	Article K.11	Article 39
TITLE IV	**TITLE IV**	Article K.12	Article 40
Article I	Article 10	Article K.13	Article 41
TITLE V (***)	**TITLE V**	Article K.14	Article 42
Article J.1	Article 11		
Article J.2	Article 12	**TITLE VIa (**)**	**TITLE VII**
Article J.3	Article 13	Article K.15 (*)	Article 43
Article J.4	Article 14	Article K.16 (*)	Article 44
Article J.5	Article 15	Article K.17 (*)	Article 45
Article J.6	Article 16		
Article J.7	Article 17	**TITLE VII**	**TITLE VIII**
Article J.8	Article 18	Article L	Article 46
Article J.9	Article 19	Article M	Article 47
Article J.10	Article 20	Article N	Article 48
Article J.11	Article 21	Article O	Article 49
Article J.12	Article 22	Article P	Article 50
Article J.13	Article 23	Article Q	Article 51
Article J.14	Article 24	Article R	Article 52
Article J.15	Article 25	Article S	Article 53
Article J.16	Article 26		
Article J.17	Article 27		
Article J.18	Article 28		

(*) New Article introduced by the Treaty of Amsterdam.
(**) New Title introduced by the Treaty of Amsterdam.
(***) Title restructured by the Treaty of Amsterdam.

B. Treaty establishing the European Community

Previous numbering	New numbering	Previous numbering	New numbering
PART ONE	**PART ONE**	Article 15 (repealed)	—
Article 1	Article 1	Article 16 (repealed	—
Article 2	Article 2	Article 17 (repealed)	—
Article 3	Article 3		
Article 3a	Article 4		
Article 3b	Article 5	**Section 2 (deleted)**	—
Article 3c (*)	Article 6	Article 18 (repealed)	—
Article 4	Article 7	Article 19 (repealed)	—
Article 4a	Article 8	Article 20 (repealed)	—
Article 4b	Article 9		
Article 5	Article 10	Article 21 (repealed)	—
Article 5a (*)	Article 11	Article 22 (repealed)	—
Article 6	Article 12		
Article 6a (*)	Article 13	Article 23 (repealed)	—
Article 7 (repealed)	—	Article 24 (repealed)	—
Article 7a	Article 14		
Article 7b (repealed)	—	Article 25 (repealed)	—
Article 7c	Article 15	Article 26 (repealed)	—
Article 7d (*)	Article 16	Article 27 (repealed)	—
PART TWO	**PART TWO**		
Article 8	Article 17	Article 28	Article 26
Article 8a	Article 18	Article 29	Article 27
Article 8b	Article 19		
Article 8c	Article 20		
Article 8d	Article 21	**CHAPTER 2**	**CHAPTER 2**
Article 8e	Article 22	Article 30	Article 28
PART THREE	**PART THREE**	Article 31 (repealed)	—
TITLE I	**TITLE I**	Article 32 (repealed)	—
Article 9	Article 23	Article 33 (repealed)	—
Article 10	Article 24	Article 34	Article 29
Article 11 (repealed)	—	Article 35 (repealed)	—
CHAPTER 1	**CHAPTER 1**	Article 36	Article 30
Section 1 (deleted)	—	Article 37	Article 31
Article 12	Article 25		
Article 13 (repealed)	—		
Article 14 (repealed)	—		

(*) New Article introduced by the Treaty of Amsterdam.

Previous numbering	New numbering	Previous numbering	New numbering
TITLE II	**TITLE II**	Article 69 (repealed)	—
Article 38	Article 32	Article 70 (repealed)	—
Article 39	Article 33	Article 71 (repealed)	—
Article 40	Article 34	Article 72 (repealed)	—
Article 41	Article 35	Article 73 (repealed)	—
Article 42	Article 36	Article 73a (repealed)	—
Article 43	Article 37	Article 73b	Article 56
Article 44 (repealed)	—	Article 73c	Article 57
Article 45 (repealed)	—	Article 73d	Article 58
Article 46	Article 38	Article 73e (repealed)	—
Article 47 (repealed)	—	Article 73f	Article 59
TITLE III	**TITLE III**	Article 73g	Article 60
CHAPTER 1	**CHAPTER 1**	Article 73h (repealed)	—
Article 48	Article 39	**TITLE IIIa (**)**	**TITLE IV**
Article 49	Article 40	Article 73i (*)	Article 61
Article 50	Article 41	Article 73j (*)	Article 62
Article 51	Article 42	Article 73k (*)	Article 63
CHAPTER 2	**CHAPTER 2**	Article 73l (*)	Article 64
Article 52	Article 43	Article 73m (*)	Article 65
Article 53 (repealed)	—	Article 73n (*)	Article 66
Article 54	Article 44	Article 73o (*)	Article 67
Article 55	Article 45	Article 73p (*)	Article 68
Article 56	Article 46	Article 73q (*)	Article 69
Article 57	Article 47	**TITLE IV**	**TITLE V**
Article 58	Article 48	Article 74	Article 70
CHAPTER 3	**CHAPTER 3**	Article 75	Article 71
Article 59	Article 49	Article 76	Article 72
Article 60	Article 50	Article 77	Article 73
Article 61	Article 51	Article 78	Article 74
Article 62 (repealed)	—	Article 79	Article 75
Article 63	Article 52	Article 80	Article 76
Article 64	Article 53	Article 81	Article 77
Article 65	Article 54	Article 82	Article 78
Article 66	Article 55	Article 83	Article 79
CHAPTER 4	**CHAPTER 4**	Article 84	Article 80
Article 67 (repealed)	—		
Article 68 (repealed)	—		

(*) New Article introduced by the Treaty of Amsterdam.
(**) New Title introduced by the Treaty of Amsterdam.

Previous numbering	New numbering	Previous numbering	New numbering
TITLE V	TITLE VI	Article 104	Article 101
CHAPTER 1	CHAPTER 1	Article 104a	Article 102
SECTION 1	SECTION 1	Article 104b	Article 103
		Article 104c	Article 104
Article 85	Article 81	CHAPTER 2	CHAPTER 2
Article 86	Article 82	Article 105	Article 105
Article 87	Article 83	Article 105a	Article 106
Article 88	Article 84	Article 106	Article 107
Article 89	Article 85	Article 107	Article 108
Article 90	Article 86	Article 108	Article 109
Section 2 (deleted)	—	Article 108a	Article 110
Article 91 (repealed)	—	Article 109	Article 111
SECTION 3	SECTION 2	CHAPTER 3	CHAPTER 3
Article 92	Article 87	Article 109a	Article 112
Article 93	Article 88	Article 109b	Article 113
Article 94	Article 89	Article 109c	Article 114
		Article 109d	Article 115
CHAPTER 2	CHAPTER 2	CHAPTER 4	CHAPTER 4
Article 95	Article 90	Article 109e	Article 116
Article 96	Article 91	Article 109f	Article 117
Article 97 (repealed)	—	Article 109g	Article 118
Article 98	Article 92	Article 109h	Article 119
Article 99	Article 93	Article 109i	Article 120
		Article 109j	Article 121
CHAPTER 3	CHAPTER 3	Article 109k	Article 122
Article 100	Article 94	Article 109l	Article 123
Article 100a	Article 95	Article 109m	Article 124
Article 100b (repealed)	—	TITLE VIa (**)	TITLE VIII
Article 100c (repealed)	—	Article 109n (*)	Article 125
Article 100d (repealed)	—	Article 109o (*)	Article 126
Article 101	Article 96	Article 109p (*)	Article 127
Article 102	Article 97	Article 109q (*)	Article 128
		Article 109r (*)	Article 129
TITLE VI	TITLE VII	Article 109s (*)	Article 130
CHAPTER 1	CHAPTER 1	TITLE VII	TITLE IX
		Article 110	Article 131
Article 102a	Article 98	Article 111 (repealed)	—
Article 103	Article 99	Article 112	Article 132
Article 103a	Article 100	Article 113	Article 133

(*) New Article introduced by the Treaty of Amsterdam.
(**) New Title introduced by the Treaty of Amsterdam.

Previous numbering	New numbering
Article 114 (repealed)	—
Article 115	Article 134
TITLE VIIa (**)	TITLE X
Article 116 (*)	Article 135
TITLE VIII	TITLE XI
CHAPTER 1 (***)	CHAPTER 1
Article 117	Article 136
Article 118	Article 137
Article 118a	Article 138
Article 118b	Article 139
Article 118c	Article 140
Article 119	Article 141
Article 119a	Article 142
Article 120	Article 143
Article 121	Article 144
Article 122	Article 145
CHAPTER 2	CHAPTER 2
Article 123	Article 146
Article 124	Article 147
Article 125	Article 148
CHAPTER 3	CHAPTER 3
Article 126	Article 149
Article 127	Article 150
TITLE IX	TITLE XII
Article 128	Article 151
TITLE X	TITLE XIII
Article 129	Article 152
TITLE XI	TITLE XIV
Article 129a	Article 153
TITLE XII	TITLE XV
Article 129b	Article 154
Article 129c	Article 155
Article 129d	Article 156
TITLE XIII	TITLE XVI
Article 130	Article 157

Previous numbering	New numbering
TITLE XIV	TITLE XVII
Article 130a	Article 158
Article 130b	Article 159
Article 130c	Article 160
Article 130d	Article 161
Article 130e	Article 162
TITLE XV	TITLE XVIII
Article 130f	Article 163
Article 130g	Article 164
Article 130h	Article 165
Article 130i	Article 166
Article 130j	Article 167
Article 130k	Article 168
Article 130l	Article 169
Article 130m	Article 170
Article 130n	Article 171
Article 130o	Article 172
Article 130p	Article 173
Article 130q (repealed)	—
TITLE XVI	TITLE XIX
Article 130r	Article 174
Article 130s	Article 175
Article 130t	Article 176
TITLE XVII	TITLE XX
Article 130u	Article 177
Article 130v	Article 178
Article 130w	Article 179
Article 130x	Article 180
Article 130y	Article 181
PART FOUR	PART FOUR
Article 131	Article 182
Article 132	Article 183
Article 133	Article 184
Article 134	Article 185
Article 135	Article 186
Article 136	Article 187
Article 136a	Article 188

(*) New Article introduced by the Treaty of Amsterdam.
(**) New Title introduced by the Treaty of Amsterdam.
(***) Chapter 1 restructured by the Treaty of Amsterdam.

Previous numbering	New numbering	Previous numbering	New numbering
PART FIVE	PART FIVE	Article 166	Article 222
TITLE I	TITLE I	Article 167	Article 223
CHAPTER 1	CHAPTER 1	Article 168	Article 224
SECTION 1	SECTION 1	Article 168 a	Article 225
Article 137	Article 189	Article 169	Article 226
Article 138	Article 190	Article 170	Article 227
Article 138a	Article 191	Article 171	Article 228
Article 138b	Article 192	Article 172	Article 229
Article 138c	Article 193	Article 173	Article 230
Article 138d	Article 194	Article 174	Article 231
Article 138e	Article 195	Article 175	Article 232
Article 139	Article 196	Article 176	Article 233
Article 140	Article 197	Article 177	Article 234
Article 141	Article 198	Article 178	Article 235
Article 142	Article 199	Article 179	Article 236
Article 143	Article 200	Article 180	Article 237
Article 144	Article 201	Article 181	Article 238
		Article 182	Article 239
SECTION 2	SECTION 2	Article 183	Article 240
Article 145	Article 202	Article 184	Article 241
Article 146	Article 203	Article 185	Article 242
Article 147	Article 204	Article 186	Article 243
Article 148	Article 205	Article 187	Article 244
Article 149 (repealed)	—	Article 188	Article 245
Article 150	Article 206	SECTION 5	SECTION 5
Article 151	Article 207	Article 188a	Article 246
Article 152	Article 208	Article 188b	Article 247
Article 153	Article 209	Article 188c	Article 248
Article 154	Article 210		
		CHAPTER 2	CHAPTER 2
SECTION 3	SECTION 3	Article 189	Article 249
Article 155	Article 211	Article 189a	Article 250
Article 156	Article 212	Article 189b	Article 251
Article 157	Article 213	Article 189c	Article 252
Article 158	Article 214	Article 190	Article 253
Article 159	Article 215	Article 191	Article 254
Article 160	Article 216	Article 191a (*)	Article 255
Article 161	Article 217	Article 192	Article 256
Article 162	Article 218		
Article 163	Article 219	CHAPTER 3	CHAPTER 3
		Article 193	Article 257
SECTION 4	SECTION 4	Article 194	Article 258
Article 164	Article 220	Article 195	Article 259
Article 165	Article 221	Article 196	Article 260
		Article 197	Article 261
		Article 198	Article 262

(*) New Article introduced by the Treaty of Amsterdam.

Previous numbering	New numbering	Previous numbering	New numbering
CHAPTER 4	CHAPTER 4	Article 216	Article 289
Article 198a	Article 263	Article 217	Article 290
Article 198b	Article 264	Article 218 (*)	Article 291
Article 198c	Article 265	Article 219	Article 292
		Article 220	Article 293
CHAPTER 5	CHAPTER 5	Article 221	Article 294
Article 198d	Article 266	Article 222	Article 295
Article 198e	Article 267	Article 223	Article 296
		Article 224	Article 297
TITLE II	TITLE II	Article 225	Article 298
Article 199	Article 268	Article 226 (repealed)	—
Article 200 (repealed)	—	Article 227	Article 299
Article 201	Article 269	Article 228	Article 300
Article 201a	Article 270	Article 228a	Article 301
Article 202	Article 271	Article 229	Article 302
Article 203	Article 272	Article 230	Article 303
Article 204	Article 273	Article 231	Article 304
Article 205	Article 274	Article 232	Article 305
Article 205a	Article 275	Article 233	Article 306
Article 206	Article 276	Article 234	Article 307
Article 206a (repealed)	—	Article 235	Article 308
Article 207	Article 277	Article 236 (*)	Article 309
Article 208	Article 278	Article 237 (repealed)	—
Article 209	Article 279	Article 238	Article 310
Article 209a	Article 280	Article 239	Article 311
		Article 240	Article 312
PART SIX	PART SIX	Article 241 (repealed)	—
Article 210	Article 281	Article 242 (repealed)	—
Article 211	Article 282	Article 243 (repealed)	—
Article 212 (*)	Article 283	Article 244 (repealed)	—
Article 213	Article 284	Article 245 (repealed)	—
Article 213a (*)	Article 285	Article 246 (repealed)	—
Article 213b (*)	Article 286	FINAL PROVISIONS	FINAL PROVISIONS
Article 214	Article 287	Article 247	Article 313
Article 215	Article 288	Article 248	Article 314

(*) New Article introduced by the Treaty of Amsterdam.

PROTOCOLS

A. PROTOCOL ANNEXED TO THE TREATY ON EUROPEAN UNION

Protocol on Article J.7 of the Treaty on European Union

THE HIGH CONTRACTING PARTIES,

BEARING IN MIND the need to implement fully the provisions of Article J.7(1), second subparagraph, and (3) of the Treaty on European Union,

BEARING IN MIND that the policy of the Union in accordance with Article J.7 shall not prejudice the specific character of the security and defence policy of certain Member States and shall respect the obligations of certain Member States, which see their common defence realised in NATO, under the North Atlantic Treaty and be compatible with the common security and defence policy established within that framework,

HAVE AGREED UPON the following provision, which is annexed to the Treaty on European Union,

The European Union shall draw up, together with the Western European Union, arrangements for enhanced cooperation between them, within a year from the entry into force of the Treaty of Amsterdam.

———

B. PROTOCOLS ANNEXED TO THE TREATY ON EUROPEAN UNION AND TO THE TREATY ESTABLISHING THE EUROPEAN COMMUNITY

Protocol integrating the Schengen *acquis* into the framework of the European Union

THE HIGH CONTRACTING PARTIES,

NOTING that the Agreements on the gradual abolition of checks at common borders signed by some Member States of the European Union in Schengen on 14 June 1985 and on 19 June 1990, as well as related agreements and the rules adopted on the basis of these agreements, are aimed at enhancing European integration and, in particular, at enabling the European Union to develop more rapidly into an area of freedom, security and justice,

DESIRING to incorporate the abovementioned agreements and rules into the framework of the European Union,

CONFIRMING that the provisions of the Schengen *acquis* are applicable only if and as far as they are compatible with the European Union and Community law,

TAKING INTO ACCOUNT the special position of Denmark,

TAKING INTO ACCOUNT the fact that Ireland and the United Kingdom of Great Britain and Northern Ireland are not parties to and have not signed the abovementioned agreements; that provision should, however, be made to allow those Member States to accept some or all of the provisions thereof,

RECOGNISING that, as a consequence, it is necessary to make use of the provisions of the Treaty on European Union and of the Treaty establishing the European Community concerning closer cooperation between some Member States and that those provisions should only be used as a last resort,

TAKING INTO ACCOUNT the need to maintain a special relationship with the Republic of Iceland and the Kingdom of Norway, both States having confirmed their intention to become bound by the provisions mentioned above, on the basis of the Agreement signed in Luxembourg on 19 December 1996,

HAVE AGREED UPON the following provisions, which shall be annexed to the Treaty on European Union and to the Treaty establishing the European Community,

Article 1

The Kingdom of Belgium, the Kingdom of Denmark, the Federal Republic of Germany, the Hellenic Republic, the Kingdom of Spain, the French Republic, the Italian Republic, the Grand Duchy of Luxembourg, the Kingdom of the Netherlands, the Republic of Austria, the Portuguese Republic, the Republic of Finland and the Kingdom of Sweden, signatories to the Schengen agreements, are authorised to establish closer cooperation among themselves within the scope of those agreements and related provisions, as they are listed in the Annex to this Protocol, hereinafter referred to as the 'Schengen *acquis*'. This cooperation shall be conducted within the institutional and legal framework of the European Union and with respect for the relevant provisions of the Treaty on European Union and of the Treaty establishing the European Community.

Article 2

1.   From the date of entry into force of the Treaty of Amsterdam, the Schengen *acquis*, including the decisions of the Executive Committee established by the Schengen agreements which have been adopted before this date, shall immediately apply to the thirteen Member States referred to in Article 1, without prejudice to the provisions of paragraph 2 of this Article. From the same date, the Council will substitute itself for the said Executive Committee.

The Council, acting by the unanimity of its Members referred to in Article 1, shall take any measure necessary for the implementation of this paragraph. The Council, acting unanimously, shall determine, in conformity with the relevant provisions of the Treaties, the legal basis for each of the provisions or decisions which constitute the Schengen *acquis*.

With regard to such provisions and decisions and in accordance with that determination, the Court of Justice of the European Communities shall exercise the powers conferred upon it by the relevant applicable provisions of the Treaties. In any event, the Court of Justice shall have no jurisdiction on measures or decisions relating to the maintenance of law and order and the safeguarding of internal security.

As long as the measures referred to above have not been taken and without prejudice to Article 5(2), the provisions or decisions which constitute the Schengen *acquis* shall be regarded as acts based on Title VI of the Treaty on European Union.

2.   The provisions of paragraph 1 shall apply to the Member States which have signed accession protocols to the Schengen agreements, from the dates decided by the Council, acting with the unanimity of its Members mentioned in Article 1, unless the conditions for the accession of any of those States to the Schengen *acquis* are met before the date of the entry into force of the Treaty of Amsterdam.

Article 3

Following the determination referred to in Article 2(1), second subparagraph, Denmark shall maintain the same rights and obligations in relation to the other signatories to the Schengen agreements, as before the said determination with regard to those parts of the Schengen *acquis* that are determined to have a legal basis in Title IIIa of the Treaty establishing the European Community.

With regard to those parts of the Schengen *acquis* that are determined to have legal base in Title VI of the Treaty on European Union, Denmark shall continue to have the same rights and obligations as the other signatories to the Schengen agreements.

Article 4

Ireland and the United Kingdom of Great Britain and Northern Ireland, which are not bound by the Schengen *acquis*, may at any time request to take part in some or all of the provisions of this *acquis*.

The Council shall decide on the request with the unanimity of its members referred to in Article 1 and of the representative of the Government of the State concerned.

Article 5

1. Proposals and initiatives to build upon the Schengen *acquis* shall be subject to the relevant provisions of the Treaties.

In this context, where either Ireland or the United Kingdom or both have not notified the President of the Council in writing within a reasonable period that they wish to take part, the authorisation referred to in Article 5a of the Treaty establishing the European Community or Article K.12 of the Treaty on European Union shall be deemed to have been granted to the Members States referred to in Article 1 and to Ireland or the United Kingdom where either of them wishes to take part in the areas of cooperation in question.

2. The relevant provisions of the Treaties referred to in the first subparagraph of paragraph 1 shall apply even if the Council has not adopted the measures referred to in Article 2(1), second subparagraph.

Article 6

The Republic of Iceland and the Kingdom of Norway shall be associated with the implementation of the Schengen *acquis* and its further development on the basis of the Agreement signed in Luxembourg on 19 December 1996. Appropriate procedures shall be agreed to that effect in an Agreement to be concluded with those States by the Council, acting by the unanimity of its Members mentioned in Article 1. Such Agreement shall include provisions on the contribution of Iceland and Norway to any financial consequences resulting from the implementation of this Protocol.

A separate Agreement shall be concluded with Iceland and Norway by the Council, acting unanimously, for the establishment of rights and obligations between Ireland and the United Kingdom of Great Britain and Northern Ireland on the one hand, and Iceland and Norway on the other, in domains of the Schengen *acquis* which apply to these States.

Article 7

The Council shall, acting by a qualified majority, adopt the detailed arrangements for the integration of the Schengen Secretariat into the General Secretariat of the Council.

Article 8

For the purposes of the negotiations for the admission of new Member States into the European Union, the Schengen *acquis* and further measures taken by the institutions within its scope shall be regarded as an *acquis* which must be accepted in full by all States candidates for admission.

———

ANNEX

SCHENGEN *ACQUIS*

1. The Agreement, signed in Schengen on 14 June 1985, between the Governments of the States of the Benelux Economic Union, the Federal Republic of Germany and the French Republic on the gradual abolition of checks at their common borders.

2. The Convention, signed in Schengen on 19 June 1990, between the Kingdom of Belgium, the Federal Republic of Germany, the French Republic, the Grand Duchy of Luxembourg and the Kingdom of the Netherlands, implementing the Agreement on the gradual abolition of checks at their common borders, signed in Schengen on 14 June 1985, with related Final Act and common declarations.

3. The Accession Protocols and Agreements to the 1985 Agreement and the 1990 Implementation Convention with Italy (signed in Paris on 27 November 1990), Spain and Portugal (signed in Bonn on 25 June 1991), Greece (signed in Madrid on 6 November 1992), Austria (signed in Brussels on 28 April 1995) and Denmark, Finland and Sweden (signed in Luxembourg on 19 December 1996), with related Final Acts and declarations.

4. Decisions and declarations adopted by the Executive Committee established by the 1990 Implementation Convention, as well as acts adopted for the implementation of the Convention by the organs upon which the Executive Committee has conferred decision making powers.

———

Protocol on the application of certain aspects of Article 7a of the Treaty establishing the European Community to the United Kingdom and to Ireland

THE HIGH CONTRACTING PARTIES,

DESIRING to settle certain questions relating to the United Kingdom and Ireland,

HAVING REGARD to the existence for many years of special travel arrangements between the United Kingdom and Ireland,

HAVE AGREED UPON the following provisions, which shall be annexed to the Treaty establishing the European Community and to the Treaty on European Union,

Article 1

The United Kingdom shall be entitled, notwithstanding Article 7a of the Treaty establishing the European Community, any other provision of that Treaty or of the Treaty on European Union, any measure adopted under those Treaties, or any international agreement concluded by the Community or by the Community and its Member States with one or more third States, to exercise at its frontiers with other Member States such controls on persons seeking to enter the United Kingdom as it may consider necessary for the purpose:

(a) of verifying the right to enter the United Kingdom of citizens of States which are Contracting Parties to the Agreement on the European Economic Area and of their dependants exercising rights conferred by Community law, as well as citizens of other States on whom such rights have been conferred by an agreement by which the United Kingdom is bound; and

(b) of determining whether or not to grant other persons permission to enter the United Kingdom.

Nothing in Article 7a of the Treaty establishing the European Community or in any other provision of that Treaty or of the Treaty on European Union or in any measure adopted under them shall prejudice the right of the United Kingdom to adopt or exercise any such controls. References to the United Kingdom in this Article shall include territories for whose external relations the United Kingdom is responsible.

Article 2

The United Kingdom and Ireland may continue to make arrangements between themselves relating to the movement of persons between their territories ('the Common Travel Area'), while fully respecting the rights of persons referred to in Article 1, first paragraph, point (a) of this Protocol. Accordingly, as long as they maintain such arrangements, the provisions of

Article 1 of this Protocol shall apply to Ireland under the same terms and conditions as for the United Kingdom. Nothing in Article 7a of the Treaty establishing the European Community, in any other provision of that Treaty or of the Treaty on European Union or in any measure adopted under them, shall affect any such arrangements.

Article 3

The other Member States shall be entitled to exercise at their frontiers or at any point of entry into their territory such controls on persons seeking to enter their territory from the United Kingdom or any territories whose external relations are under its responsibility for the same purposes stated in Article 1 of this Protocol, or from Ireland as long as the provisions of Article 1 of this Protocol apply to Ireland.

Nothing in Article 7a of the Treaty establishing the European Community or in any other provision of that Treaty or of the Treaty on European Union or in any measure adopted under them shall prejudice the right of the other Member States to adopt or exercise any such controls.

Protocol on the position of the United Kingdom and Ireland

THE HIGH CONTRACTING PARTIES,

DESIRING to settle certain questions relating to the United Kingdom and Ireland,

HAVING REGARD to the Protocol on the application of certain aspects of Article 7a of the Treaty establishing the European Community to the United Kingdom and to Ireland,

HAVE AGREED UPON the following provisions which shall be annexed to the Treaty establishing the European Community and to the Treaty on European Union,

Article 1

Subject to Article 3, the United Kingdom and Ireland shall not take part in the adoption by the Council of proposed measures pursuant to Title IIIa of the Treaty establishing the European Community. By way of derogation from Article 148(2) of the Treaty establishing the European Community, a qualified majority shall be defined as the same proportion of the weighted votes of the members of the Council concerned as laid down in the said Article 148(2). The unanimity of the members of the Council, with the exception of the representatives of the governments of the United Kingdom and Ireland, shall be necessary for decisions of the Council which must be adopted unanimously.

Article 2

In consequence of Article 1 and subject to Articles 3, 4 and 6, none of the provisions of Title IIIa of the Treaty establishing the European Community, no measure adopted pursuant to that Title, no provision of any international agreement concluded by the Community pursuant to that Title, and no decision of the Court of Justice interpreting any such provision or measure shall be binding upon or applicable in the United Kingdom or Ireland; and no such provision, measure or decision shall in any way affect the competences, rights and obligations of those States; and no such provision, measure or decision shall in any way affect the *acquis communautaire* nor form part of Community law as they apply to the United Kingdom or Ireland.

Article 3

1.   The United Kingdom or Ireland may notify the President of the Council in writing, within three months after a proposal or initiative has been presented to the Council pursuant to Title IIIa of the Treaty establishing the European Community, that it wishes to take part in the adoption and application of any such proposed measure, whereupon that State shall be entitled to do so. By way of derogation from Article 148(2) of the Treaty establishing the European Community, a qualified majority shall be defined as the same proportion of the weighted votes of the members of the Council concerned as laid down in the said Article 148(2).

The unanimity of the members of the Council, with the exception of a member which has not made such a notification, shall be necessary for decisions of the Council which must be adopted unanimously. A measure adopted under this paragraph shall be binding upon all Member States which took part in its adoption.

2.   If after a reasonable period of time a measure referred to in paragraph 1 cannot be adopted with the United Kingdom or Ireland taking part, the Council may adopt such measure in accordance with Article 1 without the participation of the United Kingdom or Ireland. In that case Article 2 applies.

Article 4

The United Kingdom or Ireland may at any time after the adoption of a measure by the Council pursuant to Title IIIa of the Treaty establishing the European Community notify its intention to the Council and to the Commission that it wishes to accept that measure. In that case, the procedure provided for in Article 5a(3) of the Treaty establishing the European Community shall apply *mutatis mutandis.*

Article 5

A Member State which is not bound by a measure adopted pursuant to Title IIIa of the Treaty establishing the European Community shall bear no financial consequences of that measure other than administrative costs entailed for the institutions.

Article 6

Where, in cases referred to in this Protocol, the United Kingdom or Ireland is bound by a measure adopted by the Council pursuant to Title IIIa of the Treaty establishing the European Community, the relevant provisions of that Treaty, including Article 73p, shall apply to that State in relation to that measure.

Article 7

Articles 3 and 4 shall be without prejudice to the Protocol integrating the Schengen *acquis* into the framework of the European Union.

Article 8

Ireland may notify the President of the Council in writing that it no longer wishes to be covered by the terms of this Protocol. In that case, the normal treaty provisions will apply to Ireland.

Protocol on the position of Denmark

THE HIGH CONTRACTING PARTIES,

RECALLING the Decision of the Heads of State or Government, meeting within the European Council at Edinburgh on 12 December 1992, concerning certain problems raised by Denmark on the Treaty on European Union,

HAVING NOTED the position of Denmark with regard to Citizenship, Economic and Monetary Union, Defence Policy and Justice and Home Affairs as laid down in the Edinburgh Decision,

BEARING IN MIND Article 3 of the Protocol integrating the Schengen *acquis* into the framework of the European Union,

HAVE AGREED UPON the following provisions, which shall be annexed to the Treaty establishing the European Community and to the Treaty on European Union,

PART I

Article 1

Denmark shall not take part in the adoption by the Council of proposed measures pursuant to Title IIIa of the Treaty establishing the European Community. By way of derogation from Article 148(2) of the Treaty establishing the European Community, a qualified majority shall be defined as the same proportion of the weighted votes of the members of the Council concerned as laid down in the said Article 148(2). The unanimity of the members of the Council, with the exception of the representative of the government of Denmark, shall be necessary for the decisions of the Council which must be adopted unanimously.

Article 2

None of the provisions of Title IIIa of the Treaty establishing the European Community, no measure adopted pursuant to that Title, no provision of any international agreement concluded by the Community pursuant to that Title, and no decision of the Court of Justice interpreting any such provision or measure shall be binding upon or applicable in Denmark; and no such provision, measure or decision shall in any way affect the competences, rights and obligations of Denmark; and no such provision, measure or decision shall in any way affect the *acquis communautaire* nor form part of Community law as they apply to Denmark.

Article 3

Denmark shall bear no financial consequences of measures referred to in Article 1, other than administrative costs entailed for the institutions.

Article 4

Articles 1, 2 and 3 shall not apply to measures determining the third countries whose nationals must be in possession of a visa when crossing the external borders of the Member States, or measures relating to a uniform format for visas.

Article 5

1.   Denmark shall decide within a period of 6 months after the Council has decided on a proposal or initiative to build upon the Schengen *acquis* under the provisions of Title IIIa of the Treaty establishing the European Community, whether it will implement this decision in its national law. If it decides to do so, this decision will create an obligation under international law between Denmark and the other Member States referred to in Article 1 of the Protocol integrating the Schengen *acquis* into the framework of the European Union as well as Ireland or the United Kingdom if those Member States take part in the areas of cooperation in question.

2.   If Denmark decides not to implement a decision of the Council as referred to in paragraph 1, the Member States referred to in Article 1 of the Protocol integrating the Schengen *acquis* into the framework of the European Union will consider appropriate measures to be taken.

PART II

Article 6

With regard to measures adopted by the Council in the field of Articles J.3(1) and J.7 of the Treaty on European Union, Denmark does not participate in the elaboration and the implementation of decisions and actions of the Union which have defence implications, but will not prevent the development of closer cooperation between Member States in this area. Therefore Denmark shall not participate in their adoption. Denmark shall not be obliged to contribute to the financing of operational expenditure arising from such measures.

PART III

Article 7

At any time Denmark may, in accordance with its constitutional requirements, inform the other Member States that it no longer wishes to avail itself of all or part of this Protocol. In that event, Denmark will apply in full all relevant measures then in force taken within the framework of the European Union.

C. PROTOCOLS ANNEXED TO THE TREATY ESTABLISHING THE EUROPEAN COMMUNITY

Protocol on asylum for nationals of Member States of the European Union

THE HIGH CONTRACTING PARTIES,

WHEREAS pursuant to the provisions of Article F(2) of the Treaty on European Union the Union shall respect fundamental rights as guaranteed by the European Convention for the Protection of Human Rights and Fundamental Freedoms signed in Rome on 4 November 1950;

WHEREAS the Court of Justice of the European Communities has jurisdiction to ensure that in the interpretation and application of Article F(2) of the Treaty on European Union the law is observed by the European Community;

WHEREAS pursuant to Article O of the Treaty on European Union any European State, when applying to become a Member of the Union, must respect the principles set out in Article F(1) of the Treaty on European Union;

BEARING IN MIND that Article 236 of the Treaty establishing the European Community establishes a mechanism for the suspension of certain rights in the event of a serious and persistent breach by a Member State of those principles;

RECALLING that each national of a Member State, as a citizen of the Union, enjoys a special status and protection which shall be guaranteed by the Member States in accordance with the provisions of Part Two of the Treaty establishing the European Community;

BEARING IN MIND that the Treaty establishing the European Community establishes an area without internal frontiers and grants every citizen of the Union the right to move and reside freely within the territory of the Member States;

RECALLING that the question of extradition of nationals of Member States of the Union is addressed in the European Convention on Extradition of 13 December 1957 and the Convention of 27 September 1996 drawn up on the basis of Article K.3 of the Treaty on European Union relating to extradition between the Member States of the European Union;

WISHING to prevent the institution of asylum being resorted to for purposes alien to those for which it is intended;

WHEREAS this Protocol respects the finality and the objectives of the Geneva Convention of 28 July 1951 relating to the status of refugees;

HAVE AGREED UPON the following provisions which shall be annexed to the Treaty establishing the European Community,

Sole Article

Given the level of protection of fundamental rights and freedoms by the Member States of the European Union, Member States shall be regarded as constituting safe countries of origin in respect of each other for all legal and practical purposes in relation to asylum matters. Accordingly, any application for asylum made by a national of a Member State may be taken into consideration or declared admissible for processing by another Member State only in the following cases:

(a) if the Member State of which the applicant is a national proceeds after the entry into force of the Treaty of Amsterdam, availing itself of the provisions of Article 15 of the Convention for the Protection of Human Rights and Fundamental Freedoms, to take measures derogating in its territory from its obligations under that Convention;

(b) if the procedure referred to in Article F.1(1) of the Treaty on European Union has been initiated and until the Council takes a decision in respect thereof;

(c) if the Council, acting on the basis of Article F.1(1) of the Treaty on European Union, has determined, in respect of the Member State which the applicant is a national, the existence of a serious and persistent breach by that Member State of principles mentioned in Article F(1);

(d) if a Member State should so decide unilaterally in respect of the application of a national of another Member State; in that case the Council shall be immediately informed; the application shall be dealt with on the basis of the presumption that it is manifestly unfounded without affecting in any way, whatever the cases may be, the decision-making power of the Member State.

Protocol on the application of the principles of subsidiarity and proportionality

THE HIGH CONTRACTING PARTIES,

DETERMINED to establish the conditions for the application of the principles of subsidiarity and proportionality enshrined in Article 3b of the Treaty establishing the European Community with a view to defining more precisely the criteria for applying them and to ensure their strict observance and consistent implementation by all institutions;

WISHING to ensure that decisions are taken as closely as possible to the citizens of the Union;

TAKING ACCOUNT of the Interinstitutional Agreement of 25 October 1993 between the European Parliament, the Council and the Commission on procedures for implementing the principle of subsidiarity;

HAVE CONFIRMED that the conclusions of the Birmingham European Council on 16 October 1992 and the overall approach to the application of the subsidiarity principle agreed by the European Council meeting in Edinburgh on 11-12 December 1992 will continue to guide the action of the Union's institutions as well as the development of the application of the principle of subsidiarity, and, for this purpose,

HAVE AGREED UPON the following provisions which shall be annexed to the Treaty establishing the European Community:

(1) In exercising the powers conferred on it, each institution shall ensure that the principle of subsidiarity is complied with. It shall also ensure compliance with the principle of proportionality, according to which any action by the Community shall not go beyond what is necessary to achieve the objectives of the Treaty.

(2) The application of the principles of subsidiarity and proportionality shall respect the general provisions and the objectives of the Treaty, particularly as regards the maintaining in full of the *acquis communautaire* and the institutional balance; it shall not affect the principles developed by the Court of Justice regarding the relationship between national and Community law, and it should take into account Article F(4) of the Treaty on European Union, according to which 'the Union shall provide itself with the means necessary to attain its objectives and carry through its policies'.

(3) The principle of subsidiarity does not call into question the powers conferred on the European Community by the Treaty, as interpreted by the Court of Justice. The criteria referred to in the second paragraph of Article 3b of the Treaty shall relate to areas for which the Community does not have exclusive competence. The principle of subsidiarity provides a guide as to how those powers are to be exercised at the Community level. Subsidiarity is a dynamic concept and should be applied in the light of the objectives set

out in the Treaty. It allows Community action within the limits of its powers to be expanded where circumstances so require, and conversely, to be restricted or discontinued where it is no longer justified.

(4) For any proposed Community legislation, the reasons on which it is based shall be stated with a view to justifying its compliance with the principles of subsidiarity and proportionality; the reasons for concluding that a Community objective can be better achieved by the Community must be substantiated by qualitative or, wherever possible, quantitative indicators.

(5) For Community action to be justified, both aspects of the subsidiarity principle shall be met: the objectives of the proposed action cannot be sufficiently achieved by Member States' action in the framework of their national constitutional system and can therefore be better achieved by action on the part of the Community.

The following guidelines should be used in examining whether the abovementioned condition is fulfilled:

— the issue under consideration has transnational aspects which cannot be satisfactorily regulated by action by Member States;

— actions by Member States alone or lack of Community action would conflict with the requirements of the Treaty (such as the need to correct distortion of competition or avoid disguised restrictions on trade or strengthen economic and social cohesion) or would otherwise significantly damage Member States' interests;

— action at Community level would produce clear benefits by reason of its scale or effects compared with action at the level of the Member States.

(6) The form of Community action shall be as simple as possible, consistent with satisfactory achievement of the objective of the measure and the need for effective enforcement. The Community shall legislate only to the extent necessary. Other things being equal, directives should be preferred to regulations and framework directives to detailed measures. Directives as provided for in Article 189 of the Treaty, while binding upon each Member State to which they are addressed as to the result to be achieved, shall leave to the national authorities the choice of form and methods.

(7) Regarding the nature and the extent of Community action, Community measures should leave as much scope for national decision as possible, consistent with securing the aim of the measure and observing the requirements of the Treaty. While respecting Community law, care should be taken to respect well established national arrangements and the organisation and working of Member States' legal systems. Where appropriate and subject to the need for proper enforcement, Community measures should provide Member States with alternative ways to achieve the objectives of the measures.

(8) Where the application of the principle of subsidiarity leads to no action being taken by the Community, Member States are required in their action to comply with the general rules laid down in Article 5 of the Treaty, by taking all appropriate measures to ensure fulfilment of their obligations under the Treaty and by abstaining from any measure which could jeopardise the attainment of the objectives of the Treaty.

(9) Without prejudice to its right of initiative, the Commission should:

— except in cases of particular urgency or confidentiality, consult widely before proposing legislation and, wherever appropriate, publish consultation documents;

— justify the relevance of its proposals with regard to the principle of subsidiarity; whenever necessary, the explanatory memorandum accompanying a proposal will give details in this respect. The financing of Community action in whole or in part from the Community budget shall require an explanation;

— take duly into account the need for any burden, whether financial or administrative, falling upon the Community, national governments, local authorities, economic operators and citizens, to be minimised and proportionate to the objective to be achieved;

— submit an annual report to the European Council, the European Parliament and the Council on the application of Article 3b of the Treaty. This annual report shall also be sent to the Committee of the Regions and to the Economic and Social Committee.

(10) The European Council shall take account of the Commission report referred to in the fourth indent of point 9 within the report on the progress achieved by the Union which it is required to submit to the European Parliament in accordance with Article D of the Treaty on European Union.

(11) While fully observing the procedures applicable, the European Parliament and the Council shall, as an integral part of the overall examination of Commission proposals, consider their consistency with Article 3b of the Treaty. This concerns the original Commission proposal as well as amendments which the European Parliament and the Council envisage making to the proposal.

(12) In the course of the procedures referred to in Articles 189b and 189c of the Treaty, the European Parliament shall be informed of the Council's position on the application of Article 3b of the Treaty, by way of a statement of the reasons which led the Council to adopt its common position. The Council shall inform the European Parliament of the reasons on the basis of which all or part of a Commission proposal is deemed to be inconsistent with Article 3b of the Treaty.

(13) Compliance with the principle of subsidiarity shall be reviewed in accordance with the rules laid down by the Treaty.

Protocol on external relations of the Member States with regard to the crossing of external borders

THE HIGH CONTRACTING PARTIES,

TAKING INTO ACCOUNT the need of the Member States to ensure effective controls at their external borders, in cooperation with third countries where appropriate,

HAVE AGREED UPON the following provision, which shall be annexed to the Treaty establishing the European Community,

The provisions on the measures on the crossing of external borders included in Article 73j(2)(a) of Title IIIa of the Treaty shall be without prejudice to the competence of Member States to negotiate or conclude agreements with third countries as long as they respect Community law and other relevant international agreements.

Protocol on the system of public broadcasting in the Member States

THE HIGH CONTRACTING PARTIES,

CONSIDERING that the system of public broadcasting in the Member States is directly related to the democratic, social and cultural needs of each society and to the need to preserve media pluralism,

HAVE AGREED UPON the following interpretative provisions, which shall be annexed to the Treaty establishing the European Community,

The provisions of the Treaty establishing the European Community shall be without prejudice to the competence of Member States to provide for the funding of public service broadcasting insofar as such funding is granted to broadcasting organisations for the fulfilment of the public service remit as conferred, defined and organised by each Member State, and insofar as such funding does not affect trading conditions and competition in the Community to an extent which would be contrary to the common interest, while the realisation of the remit of that public service shall be taken into account.

Protocol on protection and welfare of animals

THE HIGH CONTRACTING PARTIES,

DESIRING to ensure improved protection and respect for the welfare of animals as sentient beings,

HAVE AGREED UPON the following provision which shall be annexed to the Treaty establishing the European Community,

In formulating and implementing the Community's agriculture, transport, internal market and research policies, the Community and the Member States shall pay full regard to the welfare requirements of animals, while respecting the legislative or administrative provisions and customs of the Member States relating in particular to religious rites, cultural traditions and regional heritage.

D. PROTOCOLS ANNEXED TO THE TREATY ON EUROPEAN UNION AND THE TREATIES ESTABLISHING THE EUROPEAN COMMUNITY, THE EUROPEAN COAL AND STEEL COMMUNITY AND THE EUROPEAN ATOMIC ENERGY COMMUNITY

Protocol on the institutions with the prospect of enlargement of the European Union

THE HIGH CONTRACTING PARTIES,

HAVE AGREED UPON the following provisions, which shall be annexed to the Treaty on European Union and to the Treaties establishing the European Communities,

Article 1

At the date of entry into force of the first enlargement of the Union, notwithstanding Article 157(1) of the Treaty establishing the European Community, Article 9(1) of the Treaty establishing the European Coal and Steel Community and Article 126(1) of the Treaty establishing the European Atomic Energy Community, the Commission shall comprise one national of each of the Member States, provided that, by that date, the weighting of the votes in the Council has been modified, whether by re-weighting of the votes or by dual majority, in a manner acceptable to all Member States, taking into account all relevant elements, notably compensating those Member States which give up the possibility of nominating a second member of the Commission.

Article 2

At least one year before the membership of the European Union exceeds twenty, a conference of representatives of the governments of the Member States shall be convened in order to carry out a comprehensive review of the provisions of the Treaties on the composition and functioning of the institutions.

Protocol on the location of the seats of the institutions and of certain bodies and departments of the European Communities and of Europol

THE REPRESENTATIVES OF THE GOVERNMENTS OF THE MEMBER STATES,

HAVING REGARD to Article 216 of the Treaty establishing the European Community, Article 77 of the Treaty establishing the European Coal and Steel Community and Article 189 of the Treaty establishing the European Atomic Energy Community,

HAVING REGARD to the Treaty on European Union,

RECALLING AND CONFIRMING the Decision of 8 April 1965, and without prejudice to the decisions concerning the seat of future institutions, bodies and departments,

HAVE AGREED UPON the following provisions, which shall be annexed to the Treaty on European Union and the Treaties establishing the European Communities,

Sole Article

(a) The European Parliament shall have its seat in Strasbourg where the 12 periods of monthly plenary sessions, including the budget session, shall be held. The periods of additional plenary sessions shall be held in Brussels. The committees of the European Parliament shall meet in Brussels. The General Secretariat of the European Parliament and its departments shall remain in Luxembourg.

(b) The Council shall have its seat in Brussels. During the months of April, June and October, the Council shall hold its meetings in Luxembourg.

(c) The Commission shall have its seat in Brussels. The departments listed in Articles 7, 8 and 9 of the Decision of 8 April 1965 shall be established in Luxembourg.

(d) The Court of Justice and the Court of First Instance shall have their seats in Luxembourg.

(e) The Court of Auditors shall have its seat in Luxembourg.

(f) The Economic and Social Committee shall have its seat in Brussels.

(g) The Committee of the Regions shall have its seat in Brussels.

(h) The European Investment Bank shall have its seat in Luxembourg.

(i) The European Monetary Institute and the European Central Bank shall have their seat in Frankfurt.

(j) The European Police Office (Europol) shall have its seat in The Hague.

Protocol on the role of national parliaments in the European Union

THE HIGH CONTRACTING PARTIES,

RECALLING that scrutiny by individual national parliaments of their own government in relation to the activities of the Union is a matter for the particular constitutional organisation and practice of each Member State,

DESIRING, however, to encourage greater involvement of national parliaments in the activities of the European Union and to enhance their ability to express their views on matters which may be of particular interest to them,

HAVE AGREED UPON the following provisions, which shall be annexed to the Treaty on European Union and the Treaties establishing the European Communities,

I. INFORMATION FOR NATIONAL PARLIAMENTS OF MEMBER STATES

1. All Commission consultation documents (green and white papers and communications) shall be promptly forwarded to national parliaments of the Member States.

2. Commission proposals for legislation as defined by the Council in accordance with Article 151(3) of the Treaty establishing the European Community, shall be made available in good time so that the government of each Member State may ensure that its own national parliament receives them as appropriate.

3. A six-week period shall elapse between a legislative proposal or a proposal for a measure to be adopted under Title VI of the Treaty on European Union being made available in all languages to the European Parliament and the Council by the Commission and the date when it is placed on a Council agenda for decision either for the adoption of an act or for adoption of a common position pursuant to Article 189b or 189c of the Treaty establishing the European Community, subject to exceptions on grounds of urgency, the reasons for which shall be stated in the act or common position.

II. THE CONFERENCE OF EUROPEAN AFFAIRS COMMITTEES

4. The Conference of European Affairs Committees, hereinafter referred to as COSAC, established in Paris on 16-17 November 1989, may make any contribution it deems appropriate for the attention of the institutions of the European Union, in particular on the basis of draft legal texts which representatives of governments of the Member States may decide by common accord to forward to it, in view of the nature of their subject matter.

5. COSAC may examine any legislative proposal or initiative in relation to the establishment of an area of freedom, security and justice which might have a direct bearing on the rights and freedoms of individuals. The European Parliament, the Council and the Commission shall be informed of any contribution made by COSAC under this point.

6. COSAC may address to the European Parliament, the Council and the Commission any contribution which it deems appropriate on the legislative activities of the Union, notably in relation to the application of the principle of subsidiarity, the area of freedom, security and justice as well as questions regarding fundamental rights.

7. Contributions made by COSAC shall in no way bind national parliaments or prejudge their position.

———

FINAL ACT

The CONFERENCE OF THE REPRESENTATIVES OF THE GOVERNMENTS OF THE MEMBER STATES convened in Turin on the twenty-ninth day of March in the year nineteen hundred and ninety-six to adopt by common accord the amendments to be made to the Treaty on European Union, the Treaties establishing respectively the European Community, the European Coal and Steel Community and the European Atomic Energy Community and certain related Acts has adopted the following texts:

I. The Treaty of Amsterdam amending the Treaty on European Union, the Treaties establishing the European Communities and certain related Acts

II. Protocols

A. Protocol annexed to the Treaty on European Union:

1. Protocol on Article J.7 of the Treaty on European Union

B. Protocols annexed to the Treaty on European Union and to the Treaty establishing the European Community:

2. Protocol integrating the Schengen *acquis* into the framework of the European Union

3. Protocol on the application of certain aspects of Article 7a of the Treaty establishing the European Community to the United Kingdom and to Ireland

4. Protocol on the position of the United Kingdom and Ireland

5. Protocol on the position of Denmark

C. Protocols annexed to the Treaty establishing the European Community:

6. Protocol on asylum for nationals of Member States of the European Union

7. Protocol on the application of the principles of subsidiarity and proportionality

8. Protocol on external relations of the Member States with regard to the crossing of external borders

9. Protocol on the system of public broadcasting in the Member States

10. Protocol on protection and welfare of animals

D. Protocols annexed to the Treaty on European Union and to the Treaties establishing the European Community, the European Coal and Steel Community and the European Atomic Energy Community

    11. Protocol on the institutions with the prospect of enlargement of the European Union

    12. Protocol on the location of the seats of the institutions and of certain bodies and departments of the European Communities and of Europol

    13. Protocol on the role of national parliaments in the European Union

III. Declarations

The Conference adopted the following declarations annexed to this Final Act:

1. Declaration on the abolition of the death penalty

2. Declaration on enhanced cooperation between the European Union and the Western European Union

3. Declaration relating to Western European Union

4. Declaration on Articles J.14 and K.10 of the Treaty on European Union

5. Declaration on Article J.15 of the Treaty on European Union

6. Declaration on the establishment of a policy planning and early warning unit

7. Declaration on Article K.2 of the Treaty on European Union

8. Declaration on Article K.3(e) of the Treaty on European Union

9. Declaration on Article K.6(2) of the Treaty on European Union

10. Declaration on Article K.7 of the Treaty on European Union

11. Declaration on the status of churches and non-confessional organisations

12. Declaration on environmental impact assessments

13. Declaration on Article 7d of the Treaty establishing the European Community

14. Declaration on the repeal of Article 44 of the Treaty establishing the European Community

36. Declaration on the Overseas Countries and Territories

37. Declaration on public credit institutions in Germany

38. Declaration on voluntary service activities

39. Declaration on the quality of the drafting of Community legislation

40. Declaration concerning the procedure for concluding international agreements by the European Coal and Steel Community

41. Declaration on the provisions relating to transparency, access to documents and the fight against fraud

42. Declaration on the consolidation of the Treaties

43. Declaration relating to the Protocol on the application of the principles of subsidiarity and proportionality

44. Declaration on Article 2 of the Protocol integrating the Schengen *acquis* into the framework of the European Union

45. Declaration on Article 4 of the Protocol integrating the Schengen *acquis* into the framework of the European Union

46. Declaration on Article 5 of the Protocol integrating the Schengen *acquis* into the framework of the European Union

47. Declaration on Article 6 of the Protocol integrating the Schengen *acquis* into the framework of the European Union

48. Declaration relating to the Protocol on asylum for nationals of Member States of the European Union

49. Declaration relating to subparagraph (d) of the Sole Article of the Protocol on asylum for nationals of Member States of the European Union

50. Declaration relating to the Protocol on the institutions with the prospect of enlargement of the European Union

51. Declaration on Article 10 of the Treaty of Amsterdam

The Conference also took note of the following declarations annexed to this Final Act:

1. Declaration by Austria and Luxembourg on credit institutions

2. Declaration by Denmark relating to Article K.14 of the Treaty on European Union

3. Declaration by Germany, Austria and Belgium on subsidiarity

4. Declaration by Ireland on Article 3 of the Protocol on the position of the United Kingdom and Ireland

5. Declaration by Belgium on the Protocol on asylum for nationals of Member States of the European Union

6. Declaration by Belgium, France and Italy on the Protocol on the institutions with the prospect of enlargement of the European Union

7. Declaration by France concerning the situation of the overseas departments in the light of the Protocol integrating the Schengen *acquis* into the framework of the European Union

8. Declaration by Greece concerning the Declaration on the status of churches and non-confessional organisations

Finally, the Conference agreed to attach, for illustrative purposes, to this Final Act the texts of the Treaty on European Union and the Treaty establishing the European Community, as they result from the amendments made by the Conference.

Hecho en Amsterdam, el dos de octubre de mil novecientos noventa y siete.

Udfærdiget i Amsterdam, den anden oktober nittenhundrede og syvoghalvfems.

Geschehen zu Amsterdam am zweiten Oktober neunzehnhundertsiebenundneunzig.

Έγινε στο Άμστερνταμ, στις δύο Οκτωβρίου του έτους χίλια εννιακόσια ενενήντα επτά.

Done at Amsterdam this second day of October in the year one thousand nine hundred and ninety-seven.

Fait à Amsterdam, le deux octobre de l'an mil neuf cent quatre-vingt-dix-sept.

Arna dhéanamh in Amstardam ar an dara lá de Dheireadh Fómhair sa bhliain míle naoi gcéad nócha a seacht.

Fatto ad Amsterdam, addì due ottobre millenovecentonovantasette.

Gedaan te Amsterdam, de tweede oktober negentienhonderd zevenennegentig.

Feito em Amesterdão, em dois de Outubro de mil novecentos e noventa e sete.

Tehty Amsterdamissa 2 päivänä lokakuuta vuonna tuhatyhdeksänsataayhdeksänkymmentä-seitsemän.

Utfärdat i Amsterdam den andra oktober år nittonhundranittiosju.

Pour Sa Majesté le Roi des Belges
Voor Zijne Majesteit de Koning der Belgen
Für Seine Majestät den König der Belgier

Cette signature engage également la Communauté française, la Communauté flamande, la Communauté germanophone, la Région wallonne, la Région flamande et la Région de Bruxelles-Capitale.

Deze handtekening verbindt eveneens de Vlaamse Gemeenschap, de Franse Gemeenschap, de Duitstalige Gemeenschap, het Vlaamse Gewest, het Waalse Gewest en het Brusselse Hoofdstedelijke Gewest.

Diese Unterschrift bindet zugleich die Deutschsprachige Gemeinschaft, die Flämische Gemeinschaft, die Französische Gemeinschaft, die Wallonische Region, die Flämische Region und die Region Brüssel-Hauptstadt.

For Hendes Majestæt Danmarks Dronning

Für den Präsidenten der Bundesrepublik Deutschland

Για τον Πρόεδρο της Ελληνικής Δημοκρατίας

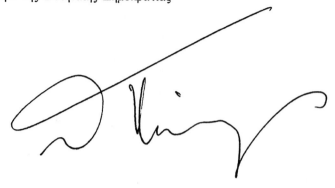

Por Su Majestad el Rey de España

Pour le Président de la République française

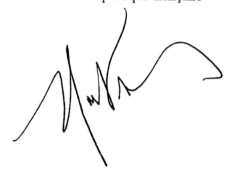

Thar ceann an Choimisiúin arna údarú le hAirteagal 14 de Bhunreacht na hÉireann chun cumhachtaí agus feidhmeanna Uachtarán na hÉireann a oibriú agus a chomhlíonadh
For the Commission authorised by Article 14 of the Constitution of Ireland to exercise and perform the powers and functions of the President of Ireland

Per il Presidente della Repubblica italiana

Pour Son Altesse Royale le Grand-Duc de Luxembourg

Voor Hare Majesteit de Koningin der Nederlanden

Für den Bundespräsidenten der Republik Österreich

Pelo Presidente da República Portuguesa

Suomen Tasavallan Presidentin puolesta
För Republiken Finlands President

För Hans Majestät Konungen av Sverige

For Her Majesty the Queen of the United Kingdom of Great Britain and Northern Ireland

DECLARATIONS ADOPTED BY THE CONFERENCE

1. Declaration on the abolition of the death penalty

With reference to Article F(2) of the Treaty on European Union, the Conference recalls that Protocol No. 6 to the European Convention for the Protection of Human Rights and Fundamental Freedoms signed in Rome on 4 November 1950, and which has been signed and ratified by a large majority of Member States, provides for the abolition of the death penalty.

In this context, the Conference notes the fact that since the signature of the abovementioned Protocol on 28 April 1983, the death penalty has been abolished in most of the Member States of the Union and has not been applied in any of them.

2. Declaration on enhanced cooperation between the European Union and the Western European Union

With a view to enhanced cooperation between the European Union and the Western European Union, the Conference invites the Council to seek the early adoption of appropriate arrangements for the security clearance of the personnel of the General Secretariat of the Council.

3. Declaration relating to Western European Union

The Conference notes the following Declaration, adopted by the Council of Ministers of the Western European Union on 22 July 1997

'DECLARATION OF WESTERN EUROPEAN UNION ON THE ROLE OF WESTERN EUROPEAN UNION AND ITS RELATIONS WITH THE EUROPEAN UNION AND WITH THE ATLANTIC ALLIANCE

INTRODUCTION

1. The Western European Union (WEU) Member States agreed at Maastricht in 1991 on the need to develop a genuine European Security and Defence Identity (ESDI) and to assume a greater European responsibility for defence matters. In the light of the Treaty of Amsterdam, they reaffirm the importance of continuing and strengthening these efforts. WEU is an integral part of the development of the European Union (EU) providing the Union with access to an operational capability, notably in the context of the Petersberg tasks and is an essential element of the development of the ESDI within the Atlantic Alliance in accordance with the Paris Declaration and with the decisions taken by NATO ministers in Berlin.

2. Today the WEU Council brings together all the Member States of the European Union and all the European Members of the Atlantic Alliance in accordance with their respective status. The Council also brings together those States with the Central and Eastern

European States linked to the European Union by an Association Agreement and that are applicants for accession to both the European Union and the Atlantic Alliance. WEU is thus establishing itself as a genuine framework for dialogue and cooperation among Europeans on wider European security and defence issues.

3. In this context, WEU takes note of Title V of the Treaty on European Union regarding the EU's common foreign and security policy, in particular Articles J.3(1), J.7 and the Protocol to Article J.7, which read as follows:

Article J.3(1)

"1.   The European Council shall define the principles and general guidelines for the common foreign and security policy, including for matters with defence implications."

Article J.7

"1.   The common foreign and security policy shall include all questions relating to the security of the Union, including the progressive framing of a common defence policy, in accordance with the second subparagraph, which might lead to a common defence, should the European Council so decide. It shall in that case recommend to the Member States the adoption of such a decision in accordance with their respective constitutional requirements.

The Western European Union (WEU) is an integral part of the development of the Union providing the Union with access to an operational capability notably in the context of paragraph 2. It supports the Union in framing the defence aspects of the common foreign and security policy as set out in this Article. The Union shall accordingly foster closer institutional relations with the WEU with a view to the possibility of the integration of the WEU into the Union, should the European Council so decide. It shall in that case recommend to the Member States the adoption of such a decision in accordance with their respective constitutional requirements.

The policy of the Union in accordance with this Article shall not prejudice the specific character of the security and defence policy of certain Member States and shall respect the obligations of certain Member States, which see their common defence realised in the North Atlantic Treaty Organisation (NATO), under the North Atlantic Treaty and be compatible with the common security and defence policy established within that framework.

The progressive framing of a common defence policy will be supported, as Member States consider appropriate, by cooperation between them in the field of armaments.

2.   Questions referred to in this Article shall include humanitarian and rescue tasks, peace-keeping tasks and tasks of combat forces in crisis management, including peace making.

3.   The Union will avail itself of the WEU to elaborate and implement decisions and actions of the Union which have defence implications.

The competence of the European Council to establish guidelines in accordance with Article J.3 shall also obtain in respect of the WEU for those matters for which the Union avails itself of the WEU.

When the Union avails itself of the WEU to elaborate and implement decisions of the Union on the tasks referred to in paragraph 2, all Member States of the Union shall be entitled to participate fully in the tasks in question. The Council, in agreement with the institutions of the WEU, shall adopt the necessary practical arrangements to allow all Member States contributing to the tasks in question to participate fully and on an equal footing in planning and decision-taking in the WEU.

Decisions having defence implications dealt with under this paragraph shall be taken without prejudice to the policies and obligations referred to in paragraph 1, third subparagraph.

4.   The provisions of this Article shall not prevent the development of closer cooperation between two or more Member States on a bilateral level, in the framework of the WEU and the Atlantic Alliance, provided such cooperation does not run counter to or impede that provided for in this Title.

5.   With a view to furthering the objectives of this Article, the provisions of this Article will be reviewed in accordance with Article N."

Protocol on Article J.7

"THE HIGH CONTRACTING PARTIES,

BEARING IN MIND the need to implement fully the provisions of Article J.7(1), second subparagraph, and (3) of the Treaty on European Union,

BEARING IN MIND that the policy of the Union in accordance with Article J.7 shall not prejudice the specific character of the security and defence policy of certain Member States and shall respect the obligations of certain Member States, which see their common defence realised in NATO, under the North Atlantic Treaty and be compatible with the common security and defence policy established within that framework,

HAVE AGREED UPON the following provision, which is annexed to the Treaty on European Union,

The European Union shall draw up, together with the Western European Union, arrangements for enhanced cooperation between them, within a year from the entry into force of the Treaty of Amsterdam."

A. WEU's RELATIONS WITH THE EUROPEAN UNION: ACCOMPANYING THE IMPLEMENTATION OF THE TREATY OF AMSTERDAM

4. In the "Declaration on the Role of the Western European Union and its Relations with the European Union and with the Atlantic Alliance" of 10 December 1991, WEU Member States set as their objective "to build up WEU in stages as the defence component of the European Union". They today reaffirm this aim as developed by the Treaty of Amsterdam.

5. When the Union avails itself of WEU, WEU will elaborate and implement decisions and actions of the EU which have defence implications.

In elaborating and implementing decisions and actions of the EU for which the Union avails itself of WEU, WEU will act consistently with guidelines established by the European Council.

WEU supports the Union in framing the defence aspects of the European Union Common Foreign and Security Policy as set out in Article J.7 of the Treaty on European Union.

6. WEU confirms that when the European Union avails itself of WEU to elaborate and implement decisions of the Union on the tasks referred to in Article J.7(2) of the Treaty on European Union, all Member States of the Union shall be entitled to participate fully in the tasks in question in accordance with Article J.7(3) of the Treaty on European Union.

WEU will develop the role of the Observers in WEU in line with provisions contained in Article J.7(3) and will adopt the necessary practical arrangements to allow all Member States of the EU contributing to the tasks undertaken by WEU at the request of the EU to participate fully and on an equal footing in planning and decision-taking in the WEU.

7. Consistent with the Protocol on Article J.7 of the Treaty on European Union, WEU shall draw up, together with the European Union, arrangements for enhanced cooperation between them. In this regard, a range of measures, on some of which work is already at hand in WEU, can be taken forward now, such as:

— arrangements for improving the coordination of the consultation and decision-making processes of the respective Organisations, in particular in crisis situations;

— holding of joint meetings of the relevant bodies of the two Organisations;

— harmonisation as much as possible of the sequence of the Presidencies of WEU and the EU, as well as the administrative rules and practices of the two Organisations;

— close coordination of the work of the staff of the Secretariat-General of the WEU and the General Secretariat of the Council of the EU, including through the exchange and secondment of personnel;

— arrangements to allow the relevant bodies of the EU, including its Policy Planning and Early Warning Unit, to draw on the resources of WEU's Planning Cell, Situation Centre and Satellite Centre;

— cooperation in the field of armaments, as appropriate, within the framework of the Western European Armaments Group (WEAG), as the European forum for armaments cooperation, the EU and WEU in the context of rationalisation of the European armaments market and the establishment of a European Armaments Agency;

— practical arrangements for ensuring cooperation with the European Commission reflecting its role in the CFSP as defined in the revised Treaty on European Union;

— improved security arrangements with the European Union.

B. RELATIONS BETWEEN WEU AND NATO IN THE FRAMEWORK OF THE DEVELOPMENT OF AN ESDI WITHIN THE ATLANTIC ALLIANCE

8. The Atlantic Alliance continues to be the basis of collective defence under the North Atlantic Treaty. It remains the essential forum for consultation among Allies and the framework in which they agree on policies bearing on their security and defence commitments under the Washington Treaty. The Alliance has embarked on a process of adaptation and reform so that it can more effectively carry out the full range of its missions. This process is aimed at strengthening and renewing the transatlantic partnership, including building an ESDI within the Alliance.

9. WEU is an essential element of the development of the European Security and Defence Identity within the Atlantic Alliance and will accordingly continue its efforts to strengthen institutional and practical cooperation with NATO.

10. In addition to its support for the common defence enshrined in Article 5 of the Washington Treaty and Article V of the modified Brussels Treaty, WEU takes an active role in conflict prevention and crisis management as provided for in the Petersberg Declaration. In this context, WEU undertakes to perform its role to the full, respecting the full transparency and complementarity between the two Organisations.

11. WEU affirms that this identity will be grounded on sound military principles and supported by appropriate military planning and will permit the creation of militarily coherent and effective forces capable of operating under the political control and strategic direction of WEU.

12. To this end, WEU will develop its cooperation with NATO, in particular in the following fields:

— mechanisms for consultation between WEU and NATO in the context of a crisis;

— WEU's active involvement in the NATO defence planning process;

— operational links between WEU and NATO for the planning, preparation and conduct of operations using NATO assets and capabilities under the political control and strategic direction of WEU, including:

  — military planning, conducted by NATO in coordination with WEU, and exercises;

  — a framework agreement on the transfer, monitoring and return of NATO assets and capabilities;

  — liaison between WEU and NATO in the context of European command arrangements.

This cooperation will continue to evolve, also taking account of the adaptation of the Alliance.

C. WEU's OPERATIONAL ROLE IN THE DEVELOPMENT OF THE ESDI

13. WEU will develop its role as the European politico-military body for crisis management, by using the assets and capabilities made available by WEU nations on a national or multinational basis, and having recourse, when appropriate, to NATO's assets and capabilities under arrangements being worked out. In this context, WEU will also support the UN and OSCE in their crisis management tasks.

WEU will contribute, in the framework of Article J.7 of the Treaty on European Union, to the progressive framing of a common defence policy and carry forward its concrete implementation through the further development of its own operational role.

14. To this end, WEU will take forward work in the following fields:

— WEU has developed crisis management mechanisms and procedures which will be updated as WEU gains experience through exercises and operations. The implementation of Petersberg missions calls for flexible modes of action geared to the diversity of crisis situations and making optimum use of the available capabilities including through recourse to national headquarters, which might be one provided by a framework nation, or to multinational headquarters answerable to WEU or to NATO assets and capabilities;

— WEU has already worked out Preliminary Conclusions on the Formulation of a Common European Defence Policy which is an initial contribution on the objectives, scope and means of a common European defence policy.

WEU will continue this work on the basis in particular of the Paris Declaration and taking account of the relevant elements of the decisions of WEU and NATO summits and ministerial meetings since Birmingham. It will focus on the following fields:

— definition of principles for the use of armed forces of the WEU States for WEU Petersberg operations in pursuit of common European security interests;

— organisation of operational means for Petersberg tasks, such as generic and contingency planning and exercising, preparation and interoperability of forces, including through participation in the NATO defence planning process, as appropriate;

— strategic mobility on the basis of its current work;

— defence intelligence, through its Planning Cell, Situation Centre and Satellite Centre;

— WEU has adopted many measures to strengthen its operational role (Planning Cell, Situation Centre, Satellite Centre). The improvement of the functioning of the military components at WEU Headquarters and the establishment, under the Council's authority, of a military committee will represent a further enhancement of structures which are important for the successful preparation and conduct of WEU operations;

— with the aim of opening participation in all its operations to Associate Members and Observer States, WEU will also examine the necessary modalities to allow Associate Members and Observer States to participate fully in accordance with their status in all operations undertaken by WEU;

— WEU recalls that Associate Members take part on the same basis as full members in operations to which they contribute, as well as in relevant exercises and planning. WEU will also examine the question of participation of the Observers as fully as possible in accordance with their status in planning and decision-taking within WEU in all operations to which they contribute;

— WEU will, in consultation where appropriate with the relevant bodies, examine the possibilities for maximum participation in its activities by Associate Members and Observer States in accordance with their status. It will address in particular activities in the fields of armaments, space and military studies;

— WEU will examine how to strengthen the Associate Partners' participation in an increasing number of activities.'

4. Declaration on Articles J.14 and K.10 of the Treaty on European Union

The provisions of Articles J.14 and K.10 of the Treaty on European Union and any agreements resulting from them shall not imply any transfer of competence from the Member States to the European Union.

5. Declaration on Article J.15 of the Treaty on European Union

The Conference agrees that Member States shall ensure that the Political Committee referred to in Article J.15 of the Treaty on European Union is able to meet at any time, in the event of international crises or other urgent matters, at very short notice at Political Director or deputy level.

6. Declaration on the establishment of a policy planning and early warning unit

The Conference agrees that:

1. A policy planning and early warning unit shall be established in the General Secretariat of the Council under the responsibility of its Secretary-General, High Representative for the CFSP. Appropriate cooperation shall be established with the Commission in order to ensure full coherence with the Union's external economic and development policies.

2. The tasks of the unit shall include the following:

   (a) monitoring and analysing developments in areas relevant to the CFSP;

   (b) providing assessments of the Union's foreign and security policy interests and identifying areas where the CFSP could focus in future;

   (c) providing timely assessments and early warning of events or situations which may have significant repercussions for the Union's foreign and security policy, including potential political crises;

   (d) producing, at the request of either the Council or the Presidency or on its own initiative, argued policy options papers to be presented under the responsibility of the Presidency as a contribution to policy formulation in the Council, and which may contain analyses, recommendations and strategies for the CFSP.

3. The unit shall consist of personnel drawn from the General Secretariat, the Member States, the Commission and the WEU.

4. Any Member State or the Commission may make suggestions to the unit for work to be undertaken.

5. Member States and the Commission shall assist the policy planning process by providing, to the fullest extent possible, relevant information, including confidential information.

7. Declaration on Article K.2 of the Treaty on European Union

Action in the field of police cooperation under Article K.2 of the Treaty on European Union, including activities of Europol, shall be subject to appropriate judicial review by the competent national authorities in accordance with rules applicable in each Member State.

8. Declaration on Article K.3(e) of the Treaty on European Union

The Conference agrees that the provisions of Article K.3(e) of the Treaty on European Union shall not have the consequence of obliging a Member State whose legal system does not provide for minimum sentences to adopt them.

9. Declaration on Article K.6(2) of the Treaty on European Union

The Conference agrees that initiatives for measures referred to in Article K.6(2) of the Treaty on European Union and acts adopted by the Council thereunder shall be published in the *Official Journal of the European Communities*, in accordance with the relevant Rules of Procedure of the Council and the Commission.

10. Declaration on Article K.7 of the Treaty on European Union

The Conference notes that Member States may, when making a declaration pursuant to Article K.7(2) of the Treaty on European Union, reserve the right to make provisions in their national law to the effect that, where a question relating to the validity or interpretation of an act referred to in Article K.7(1) is raised in a case pending before a national court or tribunal against whose decision there is no judicial remedy under national law, that court or tribunal will be required to refer the matter to the Court of Justice.

11. Declaration on the status of churches and non-confessional organisations

The European Union respects and does not prejudice the status under national law of churches and religious associations or communities in the Member States.

The European Union equally respects the status of philosophical and non-confessional organisations.

12. Declaration on environmental impact assessments

The Conference notes that the Commission undertakes to prepare environmental impact assessment studies when making proposals which may have significant environmental implications.

13. Declaration on Article 7d of the Treaty establishing the European Community

The provisions of Article 7d of the Treaty establishing the European Community on public services shall be implemented with full respect for the jurisprudence of the Court of Justice, *inter alia* as regards the principles of equality of treatment, quality and continuity of such services.

14. Declaration on the repeal of Article 44 of the Treaty establishing the European Community

The repeal of Article 44 of the Treaty establishing the European Community, which contains a reference to a natural preference between Member States in the context of fixing minimum prices during the transitional period, has no effect on the principle of Community preference as defined by the case law of the Court of Justice.

15. Declaration on the preservation of the level of protection and security provided by the Schengen *acquis*

The Conference agrees that measures to be adopted by the Council, which will have the effect of replacing provisions on the abolition of checks at common borders contained in the 1990 Schengen Convention, should provide at least the same level of protection and security as under the aforementioned provisions of the Schengen Convention.

16. Declaration on Article 73j(2)(b) of the Treaty establishing the European Community

The Conference agrees that foreign policy considerations of the Union and the Member States shall be taken into account in the application of Article 73j(2)(b) of the Treaty establishing the European Community.

17. Declaration on Article 73k of the Treaty establishing the European Community

Consultations shall be established with the United Nations High Commissioner for Refugees and other relevant international organisations on matters relating to asylum policy.

18. Declaration on Article 73k(3)(a) of the Treaty establishing the European Community

The Conference agrees that Member States may negotiate and conclude agreements with third countries in the domains covered by Article 73k(3)(a) of the Treaty establishing the European Community as long as such agreements respect Community law.

19. Declaration on Article 73l(1) of the Treaty establishing the European Community

The Conference agrees that Member States may take into account foreign policy considerations when exercising their responsibilities under Article 73l(1) of the Treaty establishing the European Community.

20. Declaration on Article 73m of the Treaty establishing the European Community

Measures adopted pursuant to Article 73m of the Treaty establishing the European Community shall not prevent any Member State from applying its constitutional rules relating to freedom of the press and freedom of expression in other media.

21. Declaration on Article 73o of the Treaty establishing the European Community

The Conference agrees that the Council will examine the elements of the decision referred to in Article 73o(2), second indent, of the Treaty establishing the European Community before the end of the five year period referred to in Article 73o with a view to taking and applying this decision immediately after the end of that period.

22. Declaration regarding persons with a disability

The Conference agrees that, in drawing up measures under Article 100a of the Treaty establishing the European Community, the institutions of the Community shall take account of the needs of persons with a disability.

23. Declaration on incentive measures referred to in Article 109r of the Treaty establishing the European Community

The Conference agrees that the incentive measures referred to in Article 109r of the Treaty establishing the European Community should always specify the following:

— the grounds for taking them based on an objective assessment of their need and the existence of an added value at Community level;

— their duration, which should not exceed five years;

— the maximum amount for their financing, which should reflect the incentive nature of such measures.

24. Declaration on Article 109r of the Treaty establishing the European Community

It is understood that any expenditure under Article 109r of the Treaty establishing the European Community will fall within Heading 3 of the financial perspectives.

25. Declaration on Article 118 of the Treaty establishing the European Community

It is understood that any expenditure under Article 118 of the Treaty establishing the European Community will fall within Heading 3 of the financial perspectives.

26. Declaration on Article 118(2) of the Treaty establishing the European Community

The High Contracting Parties note that in the discussions on Article 118(2) of the Treaty establishing the European Community it was agreed that the Community does not intend, in laying down minimum requirements for the protection of the safety and health of employees, to discriminate in a manner unjustified by the circumstances against employees in small and medium-sized undertakings.

27. Declaration on Article 118b(2) of the Treaty establishing the European Community

The High Contracting Parties declare that the first of the arrangements for application of the agreements between management and labour at Community level — referred to in Article 118b(2) of the Treaty establishing the European Community — will consist in developing, by collective bargaining according to the rules of each Member State, the content of the agreements, and that consequently this arrangement implies no obligation on the Member States to apply the agreements directly or to work out rules for their transposition, nor any obligation to amend national legislation in force to facilitate their implementation.

28. Declaration on Article 119(4) of the Treaty establishing the European Community

When adopting measures referred to in Article 119(4) of the Treaty establishing the European Community, Member States should, in the first instance, aim at improving the situation of women in working life.

29. Declaration on sport

The Conference emphasises the social significance of sport, in particular its role in forging identity and bringing people together. The Conference therefore calls on the bodies of the European Union to listen to sports associations when important questions affecting sport are at issue. In this connection, special consideration should be given to the particular characteristics of amateur sport.

30. Declaration on island regions

The Conference recognises that island regions suffer from structural handicaps linked to their island status, the permanence of which impairs their economic and social development.

The Conference accordingly acknowledges that Community legislation must take account of these handicaps and that specific measures may be taken, where justified, in favour of these regions in order to integrate them better into the internal market on fair conditions.

31. Declaration relating to the Council Decision of 13 July 1987

The Conference calls on the Commission to submit to the Council by the end of 1998 at the latest a proposal to amend the Council decision of 13 July 1987 laying down the procedures for the exercise of implementing powers conferred on the Commission.

32. Declaration on the organisation and functioning of the Commission

The Conference notes the Commission's intention to prepare a reorganization of tasks within the college in good time for the Commission which will take up office in 2000, in order to ensure an optimum division between conventional portfolios and specific tasks.

In this context, it considers that the President of the Commission must enjoy broad discretion in the allocation of tasks within the college, as well as in any reshuffling of those tasks during a Commission's term of office.

The Conference also notes the Commission's intention to undertake in parallel a corresponding reorganisation of its departments. It notes in particular the desirability of bringing external relations under the responsibility of a Vice-President.

33. Declaration on Article 188c(3) of the Treaty establishing the European Community

The Conference invites the Court of Auditors, the European Investment Bank and the Commission to maintain in force the present Tripartite Agreement. If a succeeding or amending text is required by any party, they shall endeavour to reach agreement on such a text having regard to their respective interests.

34. Declaration on respect for time limits under the co-decision procedure

The Conference calls on the European Parliament, the Council and the Commission to make every effort to ensure that the co-decision procedure operates as expeditiously as possible. It recalls the importance of strict respect for the deadlines set out in Article 189b of the Treaty establishing the European Community and confirms that recourse, provided for in paragraph 7 of that Article, to extension of the periods in question should be considered only when strictly necessary. In no case should the actual period between the second reading by the European Parliament and the outcome of the Conciliation Committee exceed nine months.

35. Declaration on Article 191a(1) of the Treaty establishing the European Community

The Conference agrees that the principles and conditions referred to in Article 191a(1) of the Treaty establishing the European Community will allow a Member State to request the Commission or the Council not to communicate to third parties a document originating from that State without its prior agreement.

36. Declaration on the Overseas Countries and Territories

The Conference recognises that the special arrangements for the association of the overseas countries and territories (OCTs) under Part Four of the Treaty establishing the European Community were designed for countries and territories that were numerous, covered vast areas and had large populations. The arrangements have changed little since 1957.

The Conference notes that there are today only 20 OCTs and that they are extremely scattered island territories with a total population of approximately 900 000. Moreover, most OCTs lag far behind in structural terms, a fact linked to their particularly severe geographical and economic handicaps. In these circumstances, the special arrangements for association as they were conceived in 1957 can no longer deal effectively with the challenges of OCT development.

The Conference solemnly restates that the purpose of association is to promote the economic and social development of the countries and territories and to establish close economic relations between them and the Community as a whole.

The Conference invites the Council, acting in accordance with the provisions of Article 136 of the Treaty establishing the European Community, to review the association arrangements by February 2000, with the fourfold objective of:

— promoting the economic and social development of the OCTs more effectively;

— developing economic relations between the OCTs and the European Union;

— taking greater account of the diversity and specific characteristics of the individual OCTs, including aspects relating to freedom of establishment;

— ensuring that the effectiveness of the financial instrument is improved.

37. Declaration on public credit institutions in Germany

The Conference notes the Commission's opinion to the effect that the Community's existing competition rules allow services of general economic interest provided by public credit institutions existing in Germany and the facilities granted to them to compensate for the costs connected with such services to be taken into account in full. In this context, the way in which Germany enables local authorities to carry out their task of making available in their regions a comprehensive and efficient financial infrastructure is a matter for the organisation of that Member State. Such facilities may not adversely affect the conditions of competition to an extent beyond that required in order to perform these particular tasks and which is contrary to the interests of the Community.

The Conference recalls that the European Council has invited the Commission to examine whether similar cases exist in the other Member States, to apply as appropriate the same standards on similar cases and to inform the Council in its ECOFIN formation.

38. Declaration on voluntary service activities

The Conference recognises the important contribution made by voluntary service activities to developing social solidarity.

The Community will encourage the European dimension of voluntary organisations with particular emphasis on the exchange of information and experiences as well as on the participation of the young and the elderly in voluntary work.

39. Declaration on the quality of the drafting of Community legislation

The Conference notes that the quality of the drafting of Community legislation is crucial if it is to be properly implemented by the competent national authorities and better understood by the public and in business circles. It recalls the conclusions on this subject reached by the Presidency of the European Council in Edinburgh on 11 and 12 December 1992, as well as the Council Resolution on the quality of drafting of Community legislation adopted on 8 June 1993 (*Official Journal of the European Communities*, C 166 of 17 June 1993, p. 1).

The Conference considers that the three institutions involved in the procedure for adopting Community legislation, the European Parliament, the Council and the Commission, should lay down guidelines on the quality of drafting of the said legislation. It also stresses that Community legislation should be made more accessible and welcomes in this regard the adoption and first implementation of an accelerated working method for official codification of legislative texts, established by the Interinstitutional Agreement of 20 December 1994 (*Official Journal of the European Communities*, C 102 of 4 April 1996, p. 2).

Therefore, the Conference declares that the European Parliament, the Council and the Commission ought to:

— establish by common accord guidelines for improving the quality of the drafting of Community legislation and follow those guidelines when considering proposals for Community legislation or draft legislation, taking the internal organisational measures they deem necessary to ensure that these guidelines are properly applied;

— make their best efforts to accelerate the codification of legislative texts.

40. Declaration concerning the procedure for concluding international agreements by the European Coal and Steel Community

The repeal of Article 14 of the Convention on the Transitional Provisions annexed to the Treaty establishing the European Coal and Steel Community does not alter existing practice concerning the procedure for the conclusion of international agreements by the European Coal and Steel Community.

41. Declaration on the provisions relating to transparency, access to documents and the fight against fraud

The Conference considers that the European Parliament, the Council and the Commission, when they act in pursuance of the Treaty establishing the European Coal and Steel Community and the Treaty establishing the European Atomic Energy Community, should draw guidance from the provisions relating to transparency, access to documents and the fight against fraud in force within the framework of the Treaty establishing the European Community.

42. Declaration on the consolidation of the Treaties

The High Contracting Parties agreed that the technical work begun during the course of this Intergovernmental Conference shall continue as speedily as possible with the aim of drafting a consolidation of all the relevant Treaties, including the Treaty on European Union.

They agreed that the final results of this technical work, which shall be made public for illustrative purposes under the responsibility of the Secretary-General of the Council, shall have no legal value.

43. Declaration relating to the Protocol on the application of the principles of subsidiarity and proportionality

The High Contracting Parties confirm, on the one hand, the Declaration on the implementation of Community law annexed to the Final Act of the Treaty on European Union and, on the other, the conclusions of the Essen European Council stating that the administrative implementation of Community law shall in principle be the responsibility of the Member States in accordance with their constitutional arrangements. This shall not affect the supervisory, monitoring and implementing powers of the Community Institutions as provided under Articles 145 and 155 of the Treaty establishing the European Community.

44. Declaration on Article 2 of the Protocol integrating the Schengen *acquis* into the framework of the European Union

The High Contracting Parties agree that the Council shall adopt all the necessary measures referred to in Article 2 of the Protocol integrating the Schengen *acquis* into the framework of the European Union upon the date of entry into force of the Treaty of Amsterdam. To that end, the necessary preparatory work shall be undertaken in due time in order to be completed prior to that date.

45. Declaration on Article 4 of the Protocol integrating the Schengen *acquis* into the framework of the European Union

The High Contracting Parties invite the Council to seek the opinion of the Commission before it decides on a request under Article 4 of the Protocol integrating the Schengen *acquis* into the framework of the European Union by Ireland or the United Kingdom of Great Britain and Northern Ireland to take part in some or all of the provisions of the Schengen *acquis*.

They also undertake to make their best efforts with a view to allowing Ireland or the United Kingdom of Great Britain and Northern Ireland, if they so wish, to use the provisions of Article 4 of the said Protocol so that the Council may be in a position to take the decisions referred to in that Article upon the date of entry into force of that Protocol or at any time thereafter.

46. Declaration on Article 5 of the Protocol integrating the Schengen *acquis* into the framework of the European Union

The High Contracting Parties undertake to make all efforts in order to make action among all Member States possible in the domains of the Schengen *acquis*, in particular whenever Ireland and the United Kingdom of Great Britain and Northern Ireland have accepted some or all of the provisions of that *acquis* in accordance with Article 4 of the Protocol integrating the Schengen *acquis* into the framework of the European Union.

47. Declaration on Article 6 of the Protocol integrating the Schengen *acquis* into the framework of the European Union

The High Contracting Parties agree to take all necessary steps so that the Agreements referred to in Article 6 of the Protocol integrating the Schengen *acquis* into the framework of the European Union may enter into force on the same date as the date of entry into force of the Treaty of Amsterdam.

48. Declaration relating to the Protocol on asylum for nationals of Member States of the European Union

The Protocol on asylum for nationals of Member States of the European Union does not prejudice the right of each Member State to take the organisational measures it deems necessary to fulfil its obligations under the Geneva Convention of 28 July 1951 relating to the status of refugees.

49. Declaration relating to subparagraph (d) of the Sole Article of the Protocol on asylum for nationals of Member States of the European Union

The Conference declares that, while recognising the importance of the Resolution of the Ministers of the Member States of the European Communities responsible for immigration of 30 November/1 December 1992 on manifestly unfounded applications for asylum and of the Resolution of the Council of 20 June 1995 on minimum guarantees for asylum procedures, the question of abuse of asylum procedures and appropriate rapid procedures to dispense with manifestly unfounded applications for asylum should be further examined with a view to introducing new improvements in order to accelerate these procedures.

50. Declaration relating to the Protocol on the institutions with the prospect of enlargement of the European Union

Until the entry into force of the first enlargement it is agreed that the decision of the Council of 29 March 1994 ('the Ioannina Compromise') will be extended and, by that date, a solution for the special case of Spain will be found.

51. Declaration on Article 10 of the Treaty of Amsterdam

The Treaty of Amsterdam repeals and deletes lapsed provisions of the Treaty establishing the European Community, the Treaty establishing the European Coal and Steel Community and the Treaty establishing the European Atomic Energy Community as they were in force before the entry into force of the Treaty of Amsterdam and adapts certain of their provisions, including the insertion of certain provisions of the Treaty establishing a single Council and a single Commission of the European Communities and the Act concerning the election of the representatives of the European Parliament by direct universal suffrage. Those operations do not affect the *'acquis communautaire'*.

DECLARATIONS OF WHICH THE CONFERENCE TOOK NOTE

1. Declaration by Austria and Luxembourg on credit institutions

Austria and Luxembourg consider that the Declaration on public credit institutions in Germany also applies to credit institutions in Austria and Luxembourg with a comparable organisational structure.

2. Declaration by Denmark on Article K.14 of the Treaty on European Union

Article K.14 of the Treaty on European Union requires the unanimity of all members of the Council of the European Union, i.e. all Member States, for the adoption of any decision to apply the provisions of Title IIIa of the Treaty establishing the European Community on visas, asylum, immigration and other policies related to free movement of persons to action in areas referred to in Article K.1. Moreover, any unanimous decision of the Council, before coming into force, will have to be adopted in each Member State, in accordance with its constitutional requirements. In Denmark, such adoption will, in the case of a transfer of sovereignty, as defined in the Danish constitution, require either a majority of five sixths of members of the Folketing or both a majority of the members of the Folketing and a majority of voters in a referendum.

3. Declaration by Germany, Austria and Belgium on subsidiarity

It is taken for granted by the German, Austrian and Belgian governments that action by the European Community in accordance with the principle of subsidiarity not only concerns the Member States but also their entities to the extent that they have their own law-making powers conferred on them under national constitutional law.

4. Declaration by Ireland on Article 3 of the Protocol on the position of the United Kingdom and Ireland

Ireland declares that it intends to exercise its right under Article 3 of the Protocol on the position of the United Kingdom and Ireland to take part in the adoption of measures pursuant to Title IIIa of the Treaty establishing the European Community to the maximum extent compatible with the maintenance of its Common Travel Area with the United Kingdom. Ireland recalls that its participation in the Protocol on the application of certain aspects of Article 7a of the Treaty establishing the European Community reflects its wish to maintain its Common Travel Area with the United Kingdom in order to maximise freedom of movement into and out of Ireland.

5. Declaration by Belgium on the Protocol on asylum for nationals of Member States of the European Union

In approving the Protocol on asylum for nationals of Member States of the European Union, Belgium declares that, in accordance with its obligations under the 1951 Geneva Convention and the 1967 New York Protocol, it shall, in accordance with the provision set out in point (d) of the sole Article of that Protocol, carry out an individual examination of any asylum request made by a national of another Member State.

6. Declaration by Belgium, France and Italy on the Protocol on the institutions with the prospect of enlargement of the European Union

Belgium, France and Italy observe that, on the basis of the results of the Intergovernmental Conference, the Treaty of Amsterdam does not meet the need, reaffirmed at the Madrid European Council, for substantial progress towards reinforcing the institutions.

Those countries consider that such reinforcement is an indispensable condition for the conclusion of the first accession negotiations. They are determined to give the fullest effect appropriate to the Protocol as regards the composition of the Commission and the weighting of votes and consider that a significant extension of recourse to qualified majority voting forms part of the relevant factors which should be taken into account.

7. Declaration by France concerning the situation of the overseas departments in the light of the Protocol integrating the Schengen *acquis* into the framework of the European Union

France considers that the implementation of the Protocol integrating the Schengen *acquis* into the framework of the European Union does not affect the geographical scope of the Convention implementing the Schengen Agreement of 14 June 1985 signed in Schengen on 19 June 1990, as it is defined by Article 138, first paragraph, of that Convention.

8. Declaration by Greece concerning the Declaration on the status of churches and non-confessional organisations

With reference to the Declaration on the status of churches and non-confessional organisations, Greece recalls the Joint Declaration on Mount Athos annexed to the Final Act of the Treaty of Accession of Greece to the European Communities.

European Union

Treaty of Amsterdam

Luxembourg: Office for Official Publications of the European Communities

1997 — 144 pp. — 17.6 × 25 cm

ISBN 92-828-1652-4

Price (excluding VAT) in Luxembourg: ECU 10